AMERICAN HERITAGE

October, 1968 · Volume XIX, Number 6

© 1968 by American Heritage Publishing Co., Inc. All rights reserved under Berne and Pan-American Copyright Conventions. Reproduction in whole or in part of any article without permission is prohibited. U.S. copyright is not claimed for color plates on pages 2, 8–12, 22–31.

MUNSON WILLIAMS PROCTOR INSTITUTE

On the day in 1832 when Mary Keys set out to paint a picture, no artist in upstate New York could have found a more fitting subject than that marvel of its time, the Erie Canal. Miss Keys, who is known today only because of this picture, painted Lockport with its famed double set of hill-climbing locks and included a packet boat with a load of overdressed passengers. An article about the vicissitudes of the canal begins on page 22.

AMERICAN HERITAGE

The Magazine of History

SENIOR EDITOR
Bruce Catton
EDITOR
Oliver Jensen
MANAGING EDITOR
Robert Lincoln Reynolds
ART DIRECTOR
Murray Belsky
ART EDITOR
Joan Paterson Kerr
ARTICLES EDITOR
E. M. Halliday
ASSOCIATE EDITORS
Robert S. Gallagher   David G. Lowe
Barbara Klaw   John L. Phillips
Douglas Tunstell
COPY EDITOR
Brenda Niemand
EDITORIAL ASSISTANTS
Mary Dawn Earley   Rosemary L. Klein
Mary A. Hawkins   Joanne Shapiro

PUBLISHER
Darby Perry

ADVISORY BOARD
Allan Nevins, *Chairman*
Carl Carmer   Louis C. Jones
Gerald Carson   Alvin M. Josephy, Jr.
Marshall B. Davidson   Howard H. Peckham
John A. Garraty   Francis S. Ronalds
Eric F. Goldman   S. K. Stevens

American Heritage Publishing Co., Inc.

PRESIDENT
James Parton
CHAIRMAN, EDITORIAL COMMITTEE
Joseph J. Thorndike
MANAGING DIRECTOR, BOOK DIVISION
Richard M. Ketchum
SENIOR ART DIRECTOR
Irwin Glusker

AMERICAN HERITAGE is published every two months by American Heritage Publishing Co., Inc., editorial and executive offices, 551 Fifth Avenue, New York, N.Y. 10017. Treasurer, George W. Breitkreuz; Secretary, John C. Taylor III. Correspondence about subscriptions should be sent to American Heritage Subscription Office, 383 West Center Street, Marion, Ohio 43302. Single Copies: $4.25. Annual subscriptions: $16.50 in U.S. and Canada; $17.50 elsewhere. An annual Index is published each spring, priced at $1.00. AMERICAN HERITAGE will consider but assumes no responsibility for unsolicited materials. Title registered U.S. Patent Office. Second-class postage paid at New York, N.Y., and at additional mailing offices.

Sponsored by
American Association for State & Local History · Society of American Historians

CONTENTS   *October, 1968 · Volume XIX, Number 6*

THE AWKWARD INTERVAL by *Laurin L. Henry* 4

DEAREST FRIENDS by *Margaret L. Coit* 8

"A CHASE UP INTO THE SKY" by *Frances Low* 14

THE ERIE CANAL PASSED THIS WAY
    Text by *Ralph K. Andrist* / Photographs by *David Plowden*   22

GRANT AND THE POLITICIANS by *Bruce Catton* 32

WHEN THE HURRICANE STRUCK by *John E. Weems* 36

HISTORY AT MIDDLE DISTANCE
A REASONABLE DOUBT by *Dan T. Carter* 40

TWO ARGONNES by *Thomas J. Fleming* 44

THE BATTLE OF THE FENCES
    A collection of posters from World War I   49

AMERICAN HERITAGE BOOK SELECTION
A FAR-FLUNG PEOPLE by *Peter Farb* 65

A BACKWARD LOOK AT THE NEW POLITICS 112

COVER: Wilhelm II, the "All Highest" but final German Kaiser, cowers before the banners of the triumphant Allies in this fine World War I poster, issued on behalf of a French war loan. Like the posters in our portfolio on pages 49–64, it is from the collection of The New Jersey Historical Society. *Back Cover:* We have taken a few liberties with this anonymous and amusing American primitive painting from the Addison Gallery of American Art at Phillips Academy, Andover, Massachusetts. Our opinions are not necessarily, may we add, those of any particular educational institution; they are merely a little crotchet of our own.

Our antiquated elective system gives an outgoing President or congressman

OUR OWN SWAN BOAT: THE DILATORY DEPARTURE

DRAWN FOR AMERICAN HERITAGE BY MICHAEL RAMUS

gregious opportunity for farewells—and mischief

THE AWKWARD INTERVAL

By LAURIN L. HENRY

OF THE LAME DUCKS

A visitor from afar not habituated to our institutions might find it odd that the strongest government on earth, having elected a new national leader, must wait ten weeks before installing him in office, leaving the old chief bereft of political power and perhaps personally repudiated, but nevertheless fully responsible for the nation's destiny in the interval. This year President Lyndon B. Johnson, who would have risked becoming a "lame duck" in the most classical sense had he sought re-election, took himself out of consideration early. His hope has been to increase his influence over events by putting himself above the campaign battle, freeing himself from fear of Election Day consequences, and eliminating suspicion of selfish political motives. It remains to be seen whether this lofty effort will be judged a success; but the complaints over his late Supreme Court appointments have already added to the generally contentious history of lame-duckery.

Among the many blessings the American people derive from our venerable constitutional arrangements, the lame-duck phenomenon stands out as a curious and possibly dangerous exception. By way of contrast, consider the British practice. If a parliamentary election changes the majority party in the House of Commons, the Prime Minister's resignation is in the sovereign's hands in a matter of hours, and within a week the leader of the new majority will be installed as Prime Minister and functioning with a cabinet of his own choice. A dramatic example occurred in 1946 during the Potsdam Conference. On July 25, Winston Churchill left the conference to go home for an election—which, to his surprise, the Tories lost. On July 28, Clement Attlee, leader of the new Labor majority, fully invested with authority, had already taken

Churchill's place at Potsdam. The parliamentary system is not guaranteed trouble-free, as the history of France and Italy attests, but when it is working in conjunction with a party and electoral system that produces a strong majority, it manages changes of governments with remarkable facility.

In the United States we wait until January 20 to carry out a decision that ordinarily is made by the voters in the first week of November. In years like this one, when the incumbent President is not running for re-election—whether by his own choice, rejection for renomination by his party, or constitutional limitation on the number of terms he can serve—the power vacuum in the White House usually appears several months before November. This recurring incapacity of the Presidency following (and sometimes before) an election has had results ranging from comic to tragic in the course of American history, and there lurks in it the possibility of genuine disaster.

Take, for example, the fateful drift toward war that occurred between November, 1860, and the inauguration of Lincoln in March, 1861 (the awkward interval was seventeen weeks in those days). Whether Lincoln could have staved off the Civil War if he had been brought to power sooner is of course debatable; perhaps by that time the conflict was indeed irrepressible. But the futility of Buchanan during those weeks, while Lincoln rusticated inscrutably in Springfield, haunts the national memory.

Or consider the plight, seventy-two years later, of Herbert Hoover, repudiated at the polls in November, 1932, but serving out his time in the White House while economic paralysis swept over the country. Hoover struggled valiantly, according to his lights, but the country regarded him as a used-up man, and Congress, under Democratic leadership, scorned his efforts. President-elect Franklin D. Roosevelt, invited by Hoover to join in an emergency effort, declined to become involved—at least on the terms of co-operation offered by Hoover. One shudders to think what might happen in 1968 should a crisis with the potentiality of blowing up the world occur between Election Day and the day of inauguration.

Our arrangements for presidential election and succession are largely a product of eighteenth-century political theory built into the original Constitution, plus early implementing legislation reflecting the conditions of political organization, transportation, and communication during the Federal period. The constitutional provisions for presidential elections were an early source of trouble, and we have patched at them intermittently ever since. We now have a hodgepodge—including original constitutional provisions, some of them archaic but others still vital and effective; early legislative decisions sanctified by 150 years of usage; crisscrossing amendments and statutes enacted as partial reforms; and myriad state laws, extralegal precedents, and party practices encrusted onto the system. Despite the troublesome characteristics of the scheme, it is built into our political system in so many ways that change is difficult.

The devotion of the framers to the principle of separation of powers led them to provide for a Chief Executive with a fixed term of four years—a system that strengthens the Presidency in some respects but provides no easy way of disposing of a President who is finished politically before his term is over. The framers sought further to make the President independent of Congress and to give him a political base in the country at large without going so far as direct national elections. Their solution was the cumbersome scheme of presidential electors, who are chosen and who vote for presidential candidates in the several states. It is left to Congress to tabulate and certify the result, break ties if necessary, and choose a President from among the top contenders if no candidate receives a majority of the electoral vote.

After the Constitution was ratified, a time schedule for the first run-through of these events was set by the old Congress in order to get the system going; before the next presidential election—which was in 1792—Congress enacted a similar schedule that endured for over a hundred years.

The statute of 1792 set the first Wednesday in December as the day for casting the electoral vote in the states, and required the states to choose their electors within thirty-four days prior to that time. The Tuesday after the first Monday in November soon became the most prevalent Election Day in the increasing number of states that chose electors by popular vote. The second Wednesday in February was specified as the day for the congressional tally of the votes cast by the so-called Electoral College.

Looked back upon in a day when one can jet to the national capital from New Hampshire or Georgia in about an hour, the original interval of a month between Election Day and the electoral vote, and that of two additional months between the electoral vote and its tally by Congress, seem absurdly long. We forget that our political forefathers had to struggle dutifully to their appointments by boat or by horse, and that thirty or forty miles a day was considered excellent progress. The typical American road had not graduated, early in the last century, far beyond an Indian path: in wet weather it was a trough of mud; in dry, a suffocating dust trap. Tree stumps left in the highway, decreed the Ohio legislature in 1804, must be not more than a foot high. When you came to a stream you looked for a ford or a boatman; failing that, you swam your horse across.

"The roads from Philadelphia to Baltimore," observed the *American Annual Register* in 1797, "exhibit, for the greater part of the way, an aspect of savage desolation. Chasms to the depth of six, eight, or ten feet occur at numerous intervals. A stage-coach which left Philadelphia on the 5th of February, 1796, took five days to go to Baltimore. . . . In winter sometimes no stage sets out for two weeks."

Under such circumstances it was not surprising that when the first Congress officially assembled under the new Constitution in March, 1789, it was over a month before enough senators had arrived in New York (then the capital) to make a quorum and tally the electoral votes of the states. As a result, it was mid-April before Washington was notified that he had been elected President. He made the trip from Mount Vernon to New York in the fast time of one week, and was inaugurated on April 30, 1789.

Quite apart from the formidable difficulties of travel, the American elective system ran into trouble very early. In 1796, it seemed fairly sure by the third week of December that John Adams would be President, but reports of intrigues among the electors contributed to lingering uncertainty, particularly concerning the Vice Presidency. In those days voters did not cast separate ballots for President and Vice President; the candidate with the highest number of electoral votes became President, while the runner-up, even if he represented a different party, became Vice President. There was apparently no complete and accurate count until the official reports from the states were opened and tallied in Congress on the specified second Wednesday in February, 1797. The result in this case showed Adams, a Federalist, with 71 electoral votes and Jefferson, a Democratic Republican, with 69. Under the original constitutional provision the Virginian became Vice President. In 1800 the electoral votes were cast on December 4, and by the twenty-third it was unofficially known in Washington that Jefferson and Aaron Burr had tied for first place. Nevertheless, the official count of the electoral vote could not occur until February 11, while Inauguration Day was legally fixed at March 4.

The long period between the casting of the electoral vote in the states and the official count in Congress thus began to look rather excessive even for those days, particularly in comparison with the short period allowed for Congress to resolve the contest, if necessary, and for the President-elect to make his way to the seat of the government by Inauguration Day. Under the legislative schedule set by the Constitution, Congress was in session from the first Monday in December until March 3, and should have been able to hold the official canvass in mid-January at the latest.

The unanticipated tie of Jefferson and Burr in 1800 provided the first opportunity for Congress to choose a President. The House of Representatives balloted from February 11 until February 17 before finally choosing Jefferson. This experience, added to the result in 1796 when the President's leading opponent had been elected Vice President, made it clear that something had to be done about the constitutional provision by which the electoral runner-up became Vice President. The Twelfth Amendment, ratified in 1804, provided for separate electoral voting for the Vice Presidency. The amendment also put March 4 into the Constitution as the permanent Inauguration Day; it did not change the schedule for the electoral process.

In the next fifty years, political and technological developments steadily made for earlier decisions and thus left an ever-lengthening gap until March 4. By 1836, moreover, the tightening of party discipline and the invention of the national nominating convention left the electors little practical alternative to voting automatically for their party's nominee, and legislation in most of the states assured that all of a state's electoral votes would go to the popular winner. Before the telegraph, a few days were required to get a reasonably accurate count of the popular vote in each state, and a few more days for reports from the states to reach Washington; but even so, a conclusive result was usually known in mid-November, nearly three months before the formality of counting the electoral vote in Congress. By the 1850's, telegraph service had sped up the vote reporting so that the identity of the President-elect was known within twenty-four hours after the popular voting was over. At the same time, the spread of railroad service made it possible for a congressman or President-elect to get to Washington from anywhere except the far West in a week. The necessity for Congress to resolve the disputed Tilden-Hayes election of 1876 was a reminder that there were contingencies for which time and constitutional processes must be provided. Even so, it was hard to justify sixteen weeks for a sequence of events that under most circumstances could be gotten through in a fortnight or less.

Of course, the rules governing the scheduling of sessions of Congress made even less sense. The Constitution provided for annual sessions beginning early in December; these ended March 3 in the odd-numbered years, sometimes in early summer in the even-numbered years. However, Congress was on a cycle of two-year

CONTINUED ON PAGE 107

Abigail Smith was nineteen when Benjamin Blyth painted her portrait in 1763, the year before she was married to John Adams.

The courtship and fifty-four-year marriage of
John and Abigail Adams was, despite
separation and war and tragedy, a moving and
highly literate love feast between two

Dearest Friends

By MARGARET L. COIT

On a cool Massachusetts morning in April, 1764, a girl named Abigail Smith watched anxiously as a Negro servant held a bundle of letters in a fire tongs over a smouldering flame. "Did you never rob a Birds nest?" she wrote her correspondent. "Do you remember how the poor Bird would fly round and round, fearful to come nigh, yet not know how to leave the place—just so they say I hover round Tom whilst he is smokeing my Letters." For they were from her suitor, John Adams, now in the second week of quarantine for a self-imposed case of smallpox, and in the first of what would be a lifetime of separations from his lady love. How much longer would they be apart? Abigail wondered. "I dare not trust my self with the thought." Meanwhile, the letters flowed back and forth between her home at Weymouth and Boston, where John's were smoked upon leaving his house, thus disinfecting them, it was believed, against spread of the infection.

This fear of the smallpox which terrorized the eighteenth century has no modern analogy. Catching smallpox "in the natural way" left eighteen per cent of its victims dead, the rest mutilated. John described two men who were recovering: one, "no more like a Man than he is like an Hog or an Horse—swelled to three times his size, black as bacon, blind as a stone," and another whose "face is torn all to Pieces, and is as rugged as Braintree Commons." The recently discovered "new method" of inoculation, which John had submitted to, was the scientific marvel of the age. The death rate was cut drastically, to 0.9 per cent, and the course of "the distempre" was light; there was little scarring.

How any rational person could hold out against this new system, John could not understand. Not that he considered inoculation a trivial matter. As he wrote Abigail: "A long and total Abstinence from every Thing in Nature that has any Taste, Two heavy Vomits, one heavy Cathartick, four and twenty Mercurial and Antimonial Pills, and Three Weeks close Confinement to an House, are, according to my Estimation of Things, no small matters.—However, who would not chearfully submit to them rather than pass his whole Life in continual Fears, in subjection, under Bondage."

Resigning himself to a lengthy separation from his farm, his garden, his law business, and his girl, John and his brother, Abigail's brother, and a group of friends, making up ten, had had themselves inoculated and retired to special quarters in Boston. "We took turns to be sick," he wrote Abigail, "and to laugh. When my companion was sick I laughed at him, and when I was sick he laughed at me." When they both were sick, the "good Humour deserted the Room." They had had their "Vomits," and the past night, he wrote Abigail, "We took the Pills you gave me." Now, they were as happy as anyone waiting for the smallpox could expect to be.

For the nineteen-year-old "Miss Nabby," the separation was almost too hard to bear. John was her "spark," her first love, at a time when eligible suitors were by no means "as plenty as herrings." But she was getting little sympathy with her tears and anxiety. For the twenty-nine-year-old John Adams was unwelcome in the home of Abigail Smith.

Who had ever heard of the Adamses? her mother demanded. The Smiths and their kinsmen, the Nortons and Quincys, had sat proudly among the ruling families of the Commonwealth since Puritan days. But Abigail's beau, stocky and blunt-featured John Adams, was the son of a cobbler-farmer, and he resembled his ancestral generations of square-set yeomen. John had done well enough at Harvard, given his humble station in life. But Abigail's mother bitterly rued the day that her older daughter Mary's acknowledged and highly eligible suitor, Richard Cranch, had brought his college friend to call.

In the time-honored manner of mothers, Mrs. Smith undoubtedly wanted better for Abigail than she had enjoyed herself. Although she was of the wealthy and influential Quincy family of Boston, her husband, William, a good pastor and farmer, was never prosperous. The little brown cottage to which she had come as a bride, and where Abigail was born, was smaller than the Adams homestead and more humble, with its pine cupboards and bare summer beams and a high-backed settle where a courting couple could seek warmth together. Life had not been too easy for Mrs. Smith; she had had to spin and wind yarn and weave sheets. Abigail was frail and fond of books; she deserved a better life than John Adams could provide.

So Mrs. Smith appealed to her husband. Could he not find a suitable husband for their talented Abby, someone more in keeping with her breeding and station? Parson Smith said nothing. Harried by both his wife and his father-in-law, the doughty Colonel Quincy, there was little he dared to say. Besides, Abigail knew what she wanted, and her father understood why. He had made it a point to talk to her young man. He liked him, liked his ideas, his views on life and love and friendship. It was too bad that he was a lawyer, of course. Law was generally believed to be a suspect if not dishonest profession. But better a good lawyer than a bad preacher. Personally, silently, Parson Smith decided that Abigail had made a good choice.

Abigail agreed. For she recognized in her outwardly cold and stolid fiancé "a Heart equally warm with my own, and full as susceptible of the Tenderest impressions. . . ." She further believed that they were "cast in the same mould," his of a harder mettle, perhaps, since she had been unable to discover "whether they have both an eaquil quantity of Steel." Both were passionate Puritans. Suffering, Abigail was convinced, was God's punishment for sins such as slaveholding. And John, although he had formally renounced the Calvinist creed, was still in the grip of its theology. "He that violates the law in any one Instance is guilty of all," he wrote, foreshadowing his later inability to appreciate the virtues of Alexander Hamilton.

Victims of snobbery, both also practiced it. John disliked most people and could not even bear the smell of the children he once taught in a country school. But

From a hill near their Braintree home, Abigail and her young son John Quincy watched part of the Battle of Bunker Hill, depicted above at the harbor by an unknown primitive artist. Charlestown was in ashes, and, as she wrote to her "Dearest Friend," she expected the British to drive the colonial forces toward her house "out over the Neck to night, and a dreadful Battle must ensue." The prospects so unnerved her that she abruptly ended her letter.

10

MASSACHUSETTS HISTORICAL SOCIETY; COURTESY *Life*

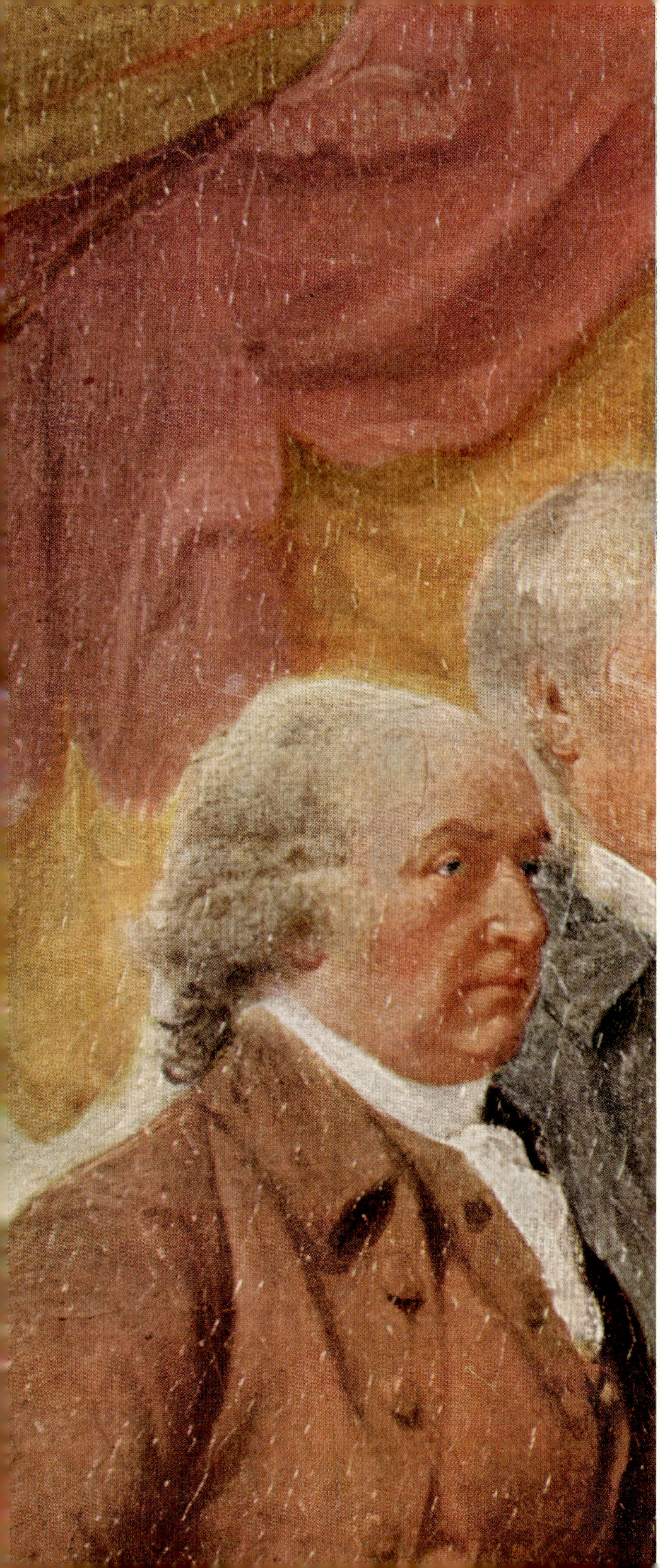

DETAIL FROM *Declaration of Independence*; YALE UNIVERSITY ART GALLERY

I am apt to believe that it will be celebrated, by succeeding Generations, as the great anniversary Festival. It ought to be commemorated, as the Day of Deliverance by solemn Acts of Devotion to God Almighty. It ought to be solemnized with Pomp and Parade with Shews, Games, Sports, Guns, Bells, Bonfires and Illuminations from one End of this Continent to the other from this Time forward forever more.

You will think me transported with Enthusiasm but I am not. — I am well aware of the Toil and Blood and Treasure, that it will cost Us to maintain this Declaration, and support and defend these States. — Yet through all the Gloom I can see the Rays of ravishing Light and Glory. I can see that the End is more than worth all the Means. And that Posterity will tryumph in that Days Transaction, even altho We should rue it, which I trust in God We shall not. —

MASSACHUSETTS HISTORICAL SOCIETY; COURTESY *Life*

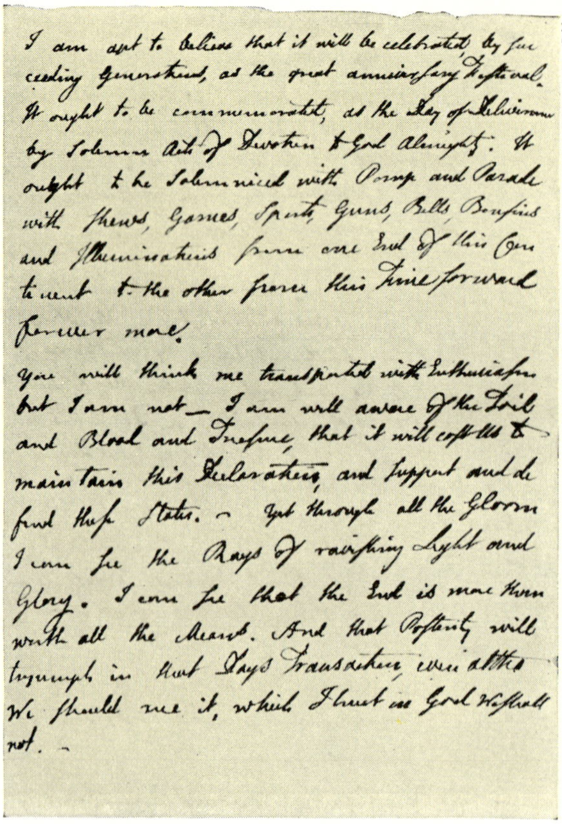

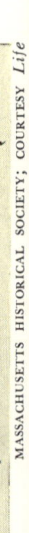

In the excerpt above, the "Day of Deliverance" that John Adams predicted to Abigail would become a national holiday of "Pomp and Parade" was actually July 2, when a resolution of independence was passed by the Continental Congress. Adams' portrait, enlarged from a one-and-seven-eighths-inch slice of John Trumbull's famous painting of the drafters of the Declaration, illustrates the delicacy of Trumbull's work.

"Love sweetens Life," he admitted; "I begin to find that an increasing Affection for a certain Lady, (you know who my Dear) quickens my Affections for every Body Else, that does not deserve my Hatred." And although Abigail once squelched a British peer with the assertion that "In our country . . . merit, not title, gives a man pre-eminence," she could write scathingly about her younger sister Betsy's choice of a small-town clergyman as a source of "mortification," so inferior was he in every way to John. (John favored the match.)

On occasion, however, John was able to convert this besetting New England sin of criticalness into loving advantage. In one letter early in their courtship, John called for kisses due from "Miss Adorable," for he had "given two or three Millions at least, when one has been received, and of Consequence the Account between us is immensely in favour of yours"; then later he chided his "Diana" upon her need "to conquer your Appetites and Passions." While still immured with the smallpox, he entertained himself at her request by enumerating a charming tongue-in-cheek "Catalogue of your Faults, Imperfections, Defects, or whatever you please to call them": You attend to cards, "that noble and elegant Diversion . . . with a very uncourtly, and indifferent, Air"; your country upbringing has apparently encouraged an innate modesty "that enkindles Blushes forsooth at every Violation of Decency, in Company, and lays a most insupportable Constraint on the freedom of Behavior"; you neither sing nor play a musical instrument; you are what "is commonly called Parrot-toed," and are ruining your health by "sitting with the Leggs across"; worst of all, your head hangs "like a Bulrush." "This Fault," he solemnly intoned, "is the Effect and Consequence of another, still more inexcusable in a Lady. I mean an Habit of Reading, Writing and Thinking. But both the Cause and the Effect ought to be repented and amended as soon as possible."

Abigail was more than equal to her lover's jesting compliment. "I thank you for your Catalogue, but must confess I was so hardned as to read over most of my Faults with as much pleasure, as an other person would have read their perfections. And Lysander must excuse me if I still persist in some of them, at least till I am convinced that an alteration would contribute to his happiness." He would not have to complain twice about her singing, "nor should you have had occasion for it now, if I had not a voice harsh as the screech of a peacock." She would lift her head, not with any hopes of appearing beautiful, but "to appear agreeable in the Eyes of Lysander." She would also refrain from sitting incorrectly, though she hardly considered it unhealthy and, she retorted, "you know I think that a gentleman has no business to concern himself about the Leggs of a Lady." The direction of her toes, she added tartly, "can be cured only by a Dancing School."

The golden light of autumn was shimmering through Massachusetts, and maple leaves blazed red against the white clapboard walls of the Old First Church in Weymouth on October 25, 1764, when Abigail Smith and John Adams became man and wife. Roguishly, her father read the text for the marriage sermon: "For John came neither eating nor drinking, and they say, He hath a devil."

They settled down in a stark saltbox house in Braintree to the normal domestic life of any young couple. John's world was a forty-mile law circuit; Abigail churned and baked and spun before the great brick cavern of the kitchen fireplace. Almost from the first, she was knitting baby clothes. Their daughter Abigail was born the following July 14, and three sons arrived within the next seven years; a second daughter died in 1770. "But what shall we do with this young Fry?" John mused in 1767. "In a little while Johnny [John Quincy] must go to Colledge, and Nabby must have fine Cloaths, aye . . . and there must be dancing Schools and Boarding Schools . . . and they wil better not have been born you know than not have polite Educations."

Success he was winning, far beyond the expectations of Abigail's family, although not of Abigail herself. His *Essay on Canon and Feudal Law,* more remarkable as propaganda than as history, with its summary of the rights of a colony that might split away, was even published in England and talked about there. Forty Massachusetts towns adopted his instructions on the hated Stamp Act. He was so prosperous that they were able to leave the farm and move into a stately white house on Cambridge's Brattle Square.

But their domestic dramas were being played out before a backdrop of oncoming war. John was often steeped in gloom; devious plots, he was convinced, were under way to injure him. The whole "execrable Project" of the Stamp Act, he genuinely believed, "was set on foot for my ruin, as well as that of America, in General, and of Great Britain." When the Crown shut down the courts as punishment for the colonies' resistance, he brooded on the end of liberty. Taxation without representation was illegal. Were the colonies a separate community, or part of the empire? If the latter, would not a majority of the empire itself fight against such taxes?

His spirits rose when Boston selected him, along with the fiery James Otis, to appear as its counsel before the Crown governor. And on a day when his two Abbys were bedded down with whooping cough, John burst into the house aglow with triumph—Parliament

CONTINUED ON PAGE 102

With Al Smith its No. 1 booster, the Empire State Building rose amid the rubble of the Depression. Is its glory at an end?

"A CHASE UP INTO THE SKY"

In an article entitled "Cloudbuster" for a 1943 issue of *WNYF*, the magazine of the New York Fire Department, Peter J. Maher reflected that "when almost everything else was coming apart and tumbling earthward with the stock market . . . the Empire State, with its gracefully curved mast 1,250 feet in the sky, became a reality." Two years later Fire Commissioner Patrick Walsh cited Maher's words in his annual report. Walsh looked back over the bleak years of the Depression and recalled the wonder and the paradox of the period from 1929 to early 1931: while the Western world was slipping deeper and deeper into economic stagnation, the Empire State Building was rising higher than any other structure in the world.

The economic skies were still bright when, at the end of August in 1929, the announcement was made that an organization headed by former Governor Alfred E. Smith would tear down the elegant but fading Waldorf-Astoria Hotel at Fifth Avenue and Thirty-fourth Street and would replace it with the world's tallest building. Six weeks later the stock market began its catastrophic plunge.

Once the slide started, many sizable ventures were abandoned, but the Empire State project did not falter. Standing behind it was a network of big-money men. Most active among them was John Jacob Raskob, who had lifted himself out of boyhood penury up through the duPont empire to become co-creator of General Motors. Other backers included Coleman duPont and his cousin Pierre, and two lesser tycoons, Ellis P. Earle and Louis Kauffman.

Alfred E. Smith, with neither money nor business experience to contribute, was drawn into the project by Raskob, who had been chairman of the Democratic National Committee in 1928, when Smith unsuccessfully challenged Herbert Hoover for the Presidency. Raskob and Smith, staunch Catholics both, had suffered side by side through bruising attacks on their religion and patriotism; now that Smith had returned to private life, Raskob was there with what he needed most—a job. Smith, like the building itself, was "up from the city streets," and he had a magnetism of legendary proportions: he would serve as front man and mascot for the project.

The August announcement followed many months of detailed planning, and preliminaries were well under way when the market crashed. Additional lots had been purchased to the west, to provide a full two-acre base. (The lot extends from Thirty-third Street to Thirty-fourth along Fifth Avenue, and more than halfway from Fifth to Sixth Avenue.) The architectural firm of Shreve, Lamb & Harmon had been retained; blueprints had been drawn, contracts let, and executive offices set up nearby at 200 Madison Avenue.

The razing of the Waldorf began on the first of October and continued despite the shock waves of October 24, Wall Street's Black Thursday. To retreat would have entailed huge losses; Raskob, with vast investments to protect, told the public that now was the time to buy stock. As the *New York Times* reported, Senator A. R. Robinson of Indiana accused him of being "psychologically" responsible for the stock market catastrophe. In December, Smith announced a loan of 27.5 million dollars from Metropolitan Life Insurance Company; the project moved on.

The Empire State Building was to become the grand champion in sky racing, New York's favorite architectural sport for some time. Two decades earlier Metropolitan itself had pulled away from the field by erecting its 700-foot Wall Street tower. But when Metropolitan offended magnate Frank Woolworth by refusing him a loan, Woolworth's pique, according to architect Cass Gilbert, led him to commission Gilbert to build a tower higher yet. The ensuing "gothic cathedral" on City Hall Park, completed in 1913, reigned as New York's tallest—at 792 feet—for sixteen years. By 1929, during a spurt of renewed competitive building, the 927-foot Bank of Manhattan Building on Wall Street appeared to be the front runner. Walter Chrysler's uptown structure, rising at the same time, was not regarded as a serious contender, but in a surprise finish a finial spire, secretly assembled inside, was shot up through its dome. At 1,046 feet, the Chrysler Building not only trounced the Bank of Manhattan; it was sixty-two feet taller than the Eiffel Tower—and was the tallest building in the world. Mr. Chrysler's victory was brief, for even as his building was opening in 1930, Empire State was under construction.

Empire State was conceived on a grander scale than the others. It was not merely to be higher; its Fifth Avenue midtown location was more commanding than its predecessors', and its site was far larger. Even without its symbolic contrast to the tumbling economic world, there was drama aplenty in the concept, scope, and execution of one of mankind's most ambitious structures.

The conception was the product, as senior architect Richmond Shreve explained, not of pure inspiration but of a symposium of owner, banker, builder, architect, engineer, and real-estate man. It had to be thus, for there were manifold problems and considerations.

Building tall would require, among other things, larger heating ducts and plumbing pipes, more and faster elevators, sturdier building columns; building tall would require extra time and extra construction equipment—and costs would mount with height.

Strict zoning laws, introduced in 1916 after the construction of the massively proportioned Equitable Building on lower Broadway, required that new buildings grow narrower as they rise. Many thereby took on a "wedding cake" profile. (Skyscrapers in later years have been granted space bonuses at higher floors in return for setbacks at street levels, and the more streamlined shaft form has become common.)

The zoning regulations meant, in the case of Empire State, that floors above the thirtieth could be no larger than one quarter of the ground lot. But the building's planners decided to forgo the use of the full area permitted; they designed the tower section to rise not from the thirtieth floor but from the fifth.

The first five floors were to be built out to the lot line. Floors from the sixth upward, eased with abutments, formed a relatively slender skyscraper shaft. The tower floors would have the so-called skyscraper advantages of more windows and minimized interior darkness. Although there would be fewer square feet of rentable space, there would also be less, by definition, to build and maintain; the tower footage was considered prestige space that would command good prices.

The original plan called for a struc-

By FRANCES LOW

ture of eighty-six floors topped by an observation platform; it would stand 1,050 feet high. That would give Empire State nine more rentable floors than Chrysler, but only a four-foot advantage over Chrysler and its surprise spire. Raskob, worried that the edge was too scant, insisted that "this building needs a hat." In December of 1929 he came up with a surprise of his own—plans for a two-hundred-foot mooring mast for dirigibles.

Some found the scheme risible. "If you know how to hold down the tail of a dirigible," volunteered the New York *Telegram*, "former Governor Alfred E. Smith may give you a job. . . ." But, first as an idea and later as a fact, the mast held the public's attention. Its record as a functioning mooring was not prepossessing, but there were, in fact, two connections a few months after the building opened. On September 15, 1931, a privately owned dirigible tied up—in a forty-mile wind—for three precarious minutes. Two weeks later a Navy blimp idled overhead long enough to produce the *Times* headline: BLIMP LANDS PAPERS ON EMPIRE STATE MAST.

The mast gradually fattened into a hollow tower with a second observation deck; it gave the completed Empire State 102 stories and a height of 1,250 feet.

Crucial to the basic plan was the matter of elevators, a vital consideration in any high construction. The need to transport 16,000 office workers and 35,000 visitors every day presented a number of engineering problems. Empire State's solution was to group the elevators in a cylindrical well that also accommodated staircases, cable shafts, utility lines, and mail chutes. The plan called for fifty-eight elevators at the base. They were divided into a number of groups, each

The construction photographs accompanying this article (all of which came from the George Eastman House in Rochester, New York) were taken by Lewis Hine, the famous photographic chronicler of America's technological society. In earlier years he documented the bewilderment of immigrants and the plight of slum dwellers; but his work with the Empire State Building was celebratory: he admired the vigor of workers like the man at left "riding the hook."

of which was to service a particular block of the building's first eighty floors. Two locals would run from the eightieth to the eighty-sixth floor, and another would shuttle up the tower. There would be twelve others: six for freight and six for spot duty wherever passenger traffic became too heavy.

The elevators would move through seven miles of shafts and would be able to handle some 1,390 persons at a time. The top speed then allowed was seven hundred feet per minute; the regulations have been eased since, and now Empire State's elevators run at speeds of up to 1,200 feet per minute.

Structurally, Empire State, basically a steel cage, was not innovative; "the latest and largest skyscraper marks only a quantitative advance," remarked architect James Marston Fitch in 1947, ". . . the first one was practically as efficient as the last." But Empire State did have a few contributions to make. Windows were applied to exterior walls with thin metal brackets instead of being set back into stone frames, adding substantially to the rentable space. This method also halved the stonework around the windows and eliminated the shadows that gave other skyscrapers a checkered appearance. Metal strips were applied vertically from window to window all the way up, enforcing the soaring, shining look.

Once planned, the construction was speeded by "the discipline of a most rigorous accountancy to the owner," according to Colonel W. A. Starrett of Starrett Brothers and Eken, the firm that had contracted to build Empire State. What he meant was that the building went up in a hurry to keep costs down.

On October 1, 1929, a truck rolled through the main door of the old Waldorf, and the demolition began. A dry-eyed Smith proclaimed that the hotel, historic as it might have been, had to come down in "the march of progress." The hotel's treasures were put up for auction, but demand was light. Some sixteen thousand truckloads of debris were carted away; "five miles beyond Sandy Hook," noted Starrett, "the remains of the Waldorf-Astoria were dumped into the sea." A seven-hundred-man crew, with derricks, compressors, and oxyacetylene burners, worked into

the winter to finish off the old dowager.

The aim was to raise the new building within twenty months. An overlapping schedule was set up: demolition, October, 1929, to February, 1930; excavation, January to March; structural steel, March to September; exterior masonry, June to December; metal window frames, May to January, 1931; elevators and mail chutes, May to February; interior partitions, June to February; painting and revolving doors, March to occupancy.

At a depth of thirty-five feet, the new basement was only five feet deeper than the Waldorf's. It had footings for 210 steel and concrete columns that would go down to bedrock. Every stage of the excavation-construction process was well timed and publicized: the first steel piers were sunk on Saint Patrick's Day, 1930.

With spring, work on the skeleton began in earnest. Empire State absorbed fifty-seven thousand tons of steel—nearly three times as much as the Chrysler Building and enough, said the corporation's brochures, to make a double railroad track to Baltimore.

The steel was poured and set into girders in Pittsburgh. The girders were then sped to a waterfront supply yard in New Jersey, whence they were trucked to the building site, lifted in bundles on cobweblike cables, and set in place. Often the whole process took a mere eighty hours. Sixteen electrically driven derricks were equipped with automatic hoists, an innovation born of an accident during the Chrysler construction in which a derrick operator, knocked unconscious by a flying brick, had dropped his bundle of steel. Despite the improvement, Empire State could not match Chrysler's record of only one life lost during construction. According to the New York *Daily News,* fourteen men were killed in various kinds of mishaps during the raising of Empire State.

Fitting-up gangs and raising gangs moved the steel up to the riveting gangs at the ever-heightening top; a heater, a bucker-up, a sticker-in, and two riveters fastened each girder with bone-rattling machines. At peak construction, thirty-eight riveting gangs were on the job; three hundred steelworkers, interchanging their posts, put the giant frame together.

The press lavished praise and admiration on the steelworkers, calling them "the poet builders" and "the sky boys who ride the ball to the 90th floor or higher, and defy death to the staccato chattering of a pneumatic riveting-hammer." Said the *Literary Digest* in May of 1931: "Like little spiders they toiled, spinning a fabric of steel against the sky . . . weaving a web that was to stretch farther heavenward than"—unhappy basis of comparison—"the ancient Tower of Babel." The pictures accompanying this article are proof that the steelworkers captivated photographer Lewis Hine. He called them "the spirit of the skyscraper," whose "experiences have given me a new zest of high adventure."

The steel men represented a multitude of ethnic backgrounds, and were union and nonunion alike; but they worked quickly. "The first column was set on April 7, 1930," wrote Colonel Starrett with justifiable pride, "and twenty-five weeks later over 57,000 tons of steel had been topped out . . . 87 stories above the sub-basement level, 12 days ahead of schedule." September of 1930 saw, in fact, two topping-out celebrations. Down at street level Al Smith laid the cornerstone, while high in the sky a handful of steelworkers, perched on a girder over the eighty-fifth floor, raised the American flag 1,048 feet above Fifth Avenue.

Other crews in the construction process swarmed in on the heels of the steel setters. Stairways rose through the skeleton; then came the electric cables and various kinds of piping, the building's veins and arteries. The lower floors were plastered before the roof was made tight. The overlapping schedule was working well, and, with the omnipresent pressure for speed, it all gave, in the *Times*'s felicitous phrase, the impression of "a chase up into the sky."

The concrete floor arches quickly followed the steel. As Starrett wrote:

Early in October, 1930, the arches of the eighty-sixth floor . . . were completed. . . . about three million square feet of arches had been set. These arches required 62,000 cubic yards of anthracite cinder concrete and nearly three million feet of reinforcing mesh. . . .

As soon as this work [had been] thoroughly organized above the sixth floor, the stone setting and outside wall construction progressed at the rate of a story a day. . . . All stonework except a few ornamental features around the lower floors were set in 113 days.

The logistical problem of how to handle all the building materials was resolved by the installation of a unique horizontal and vertical railway. Trucks drove into the site at ground level and unloaded the materials—everything but the steel handled by hoists—into twenty rail cars. The cars glided on tracks into specially designed temporary elevators, which carried them to the proper floors. Tracks, shunts, and turntables had been installed on each floor—the materials were deposited at the workers' very elbows. The system was orderly and safe; it kept wastage to a minimum and allowed New York to get on with its business without blocked streets or sidewalks.

The work force became a small army during the peak months of spring and summer, 1930. On busy days Starrett Brothers and Eken had 1,900 men on their payroll, and sixty-seven subcontractors had another 1,500 on theirs. Colonel Starrett later estimated that seven million man-hours went into the building of Empire State. In addition to the tradesmen—carpenters, bricklayers, electricians, plumbers, heating and ventilating men—there were inspectors, foremen, checkers, clerks, and even men with watering cans to settle the dust.

The care and feeding of well over 3,000 workers was a problem all by itself. When the noon whistle blew, five mobile cafeterias began shuttling up and down the scaffolding. For forty cents—and with no time lost—a man could sit on a girder and gulp down two sandwiches, coffee or milk, and pie. Ten miles of temporary piping, at a cost of twenty-five thousand dollars, brought water to virtually every man aloft. Down below there were nurses and medical facilities.

As the months went by and the building began to look like a building, sidewalk crowds, swelled by men and women out of jobs, watched in fascination. Oftener than not, the question they asked each other was, "How will it be filled?"

Opening day, May 1, 1931, was all that the promoters could have wished. The *Times* spoke of the "blue haze of a cloudless sky," and special guests at the top were impressed when told that one could see for eighty miles.

The ceremonies were a predictable political potpourri. President Hoover, welcoming a bright spot in the gloom of the deepening Depression, flicked a switch in Washington that illuminated Smith's New York tower. Governor Franklin Roosevelt came down from Albany. Jaunty Jimmy Walker, mayor of New York, remarked cryptically that the building looked like just the place where "some public official might like to come and hide."

Smith introduced speakers over the "raddio," and telegrams were sent from the world's highest dispatch station. Smith read a cable from architect William Lamb, who was in a relaxed and jovial mood on a sea voyage: "One day out and I can still see the building." Again the press sang paeans, calling Empire State "poetry in steel," "building in excelsis," and "the tallest arrow in Manhattan's quiver."

Al Smith, along with his tall, black governor's chair and his political cartoons, moved into his offices on the thirty-second floor. He was the source of an ever-freshening stream of publicity designed to keep the building before the eyes of the public—and the eyes of prospective renters. Smith's every move was news. He entertained celebrities, from royalty to movie stars to downright crackpots, in the Empire State Club and on the observation decks. When one timorous elevator rider asked whether she could expect to go up or down, Smith assured her, "It all depends what kind of life you've led."

Filling nearly two million square feet of rentable space was no small order. Potential lessees were lured by the centrality of the location and by the distinction of the site. (Huge advertisements in the press, playing up William Astor's purchase of the ground in 1827, burbled on about the "perpetual prestige" of the address.) Some ads also carried pictures

Hine found "human spirit" in the Empire State's building: the man on the right, eighty-five stories up, typifies Hine's "sky boys" in his concern for nothing but his job, in his casual obliviousness to the vista—and the danger —that lay around and beneath him.

Astor private homes, of Astor family weddings, and of the Waldorf-Astoria Hotel itself—all to "recapture an age of elegance" and to encourage occupancy at "the world's most distinguished address."

The suites ranged in size from six hundred square feet to whole lower floors of seventy-one thousand, all offered at "bargain prices because mass produced." But it was slow going, getting people to take space. Vaudeville artists enlivened their routines with sketches on "The Empty State Building," "The 102-Story Blunder," and "Smith's Folly." The bravest boasts claimed only 46 per cent occupancy when the building opened and only about two-thirds of capacity during its early years. When the King of Siam visited Empire State he said he felt right at home because his country had its white elephants too.

Smith manned the helm for the thirteen years that were the building's first and his last. Although he enjoyed his new role and remained the hero of millions, those years were underscored by bitterness, and he was often "poor Al" instead of "the Happy Warrior." On top of the stinging defeat of 1928 had come the Depression itself. Close friends went bankrupt, and some of them committed suicide. Despite his annual salary of $50,000, Smith had to battle various creditors.

During his period of managing the Empire State, Smith himself changed. He moved his residence to Fifth Avenue and exchanged his brown derby for a top hat. The once-proud alumnus of F.F.M. (Fulton Fish Market) became the recipient of honorary degrees from several universities. The former antitrust campaigner, now struggling to reduce taxes and to attract tenants, sided more and more with the men of Wall Street. Opposing the "socialistic bureaucrats indulging in communistic planning and crackpot reforms" of the New Deal, Smith saw hope for the nation only in the "initiative, [the] force, [the] foursquare, down-rightness and hard-bitten self-reliance of men of this type rebuilding prosperity."

"To fill vacant floors in the Empire State Building," wrote Robert Moses, "the Governor had to make a humiliating journey to Canossa." Smith went to Washington in 1941 and with President Roosevelt's help was able to secure the rental of sixtieth-floor suites by the Department of Commerce.

But even during those early hard times, the one-hundred-and-second-floor tower—"as high as you can get without actually flying"—was a smash hit. It attracted over a million visitors annually, and their admission dollars helped out. There was no doubt about it: the world up there *was* different. The pressure of swirling winds made snow seem to fall up, and rain turned red from the skyglow. In bad weather the top of the building was literally lost in the clouds; on calm nights, in later years when the top third was floodlit, the Empire State held regal command over the city.

In time, skating troupes, bathing beauties, circus acrobats, and mediums (who wanted to be closer to the spirit world) all performed on the observation decks. A Hollywood film showed King Kong at the literal height of his career. Health nuts climbed the building's 1,860 steps despite discouraging frowns from a management fearful of heart attacks. The building had its share of excitement—there were minor fires and periodic shootings, and there were the inevitable suicides. One of the first was headlined in the *Mirror*: PRETTY IRMA, SHE LEAPED FOR LOVE FROM THE WORLD'S HIGHEST BUILDING. Suicide rails were installed around the observation decks in 1947.

When Smith died in 1944, much of the fun died with him, but so did the hard times of depression and war. Empire State entered an era of peace and plenty; the city's office occupancy rate rose above 98 per cent, and the vast corridors in the sky, dark and empty for so many years, kindled with light and business.

Barely out of financial trouble, the building that had had little success in mooring dirigibles came into tragic contact with another type of aircraft. At 9:49 on the drizzly, misty morning of July 28, 1945, an Army B-25 crashed into the north side of the cloud-shrouded colossus. It tore a jagged eighteen-by-twenty-foot hole between the seventy-eighth and seventy-ninth floors and spewed flaming gasoline five stories up and down.

One of the plane's engine's shot across the seventy-eighth floor, ripped through the south side of the building, and wound up in a sculptor's studio on the opposite side of Thirty-third Street. The other motor, along with part of the landing gear, crashed into an elevator shaft and landed atop an empty car, which then plunged to the subcellar, touching off another fire.

The crash had also weakened the cables of another elevator—carrying two women. The cables snapped, and the car fell seventy-five stories, but its slowing devices were still operative; though badly injured, both passengers survived.

Fire fighters were able to take elevators to the sixty-seventh floor, but they had to hoof it from there. "It is difficult," said the fire commissioner's report, "to fight a blistering hot gasoline fire after plodding up eleven or twelve flights of stairs, encumbered with rubber clothing, weighted down with heavy rolls of hose."

Fourteen people were killed in the accident: eleven workers trapped in the Catholic War Relief offices on the seventy-ninth floor, and the pilot and two military passengers aboard the B-25. The death toll might have been much higher but for the fact that the seventy-eighth floor was unoccupied—and that July 28, 1945, was a Saturday.

It took twelve months and nearly one million dollars to repair the building. The work had hardly been completed when the elevator operators went on strike. Some determined tenants climbed the stairs to their offices. One day a group of brokers on the thirty-first floor sent out for lunch—which included 150 sandwiches—and tipped the delivery man seventy-five dollars. One man spent three days in his sixty-eighth-floor office waiting for an important phone call (he got it).

In 1950 the Empire State Building grew another 222 feet with the addition of a television tower that could accommodate transmitting antennas for all of New York's channels. (In 1965 a master
CONTINUED ON PAGE 80

The riveting gang on the right takes its ease nearly a quarter of a mile up, in Empire State's tower-to-be. For some shots Hine used a basket that could be swung out from the building's frame.

When the Erie Canal was built in the 1820's, it was the engineering marvel of its time. And, considering the tools and technology of the period, it still appears a rather respectable undertaking. Extending for 363 miles, stepping up hill and down valley a total of nearly seven hundred vertical feet by eighty-four lift locks, soaring across rivers on arched aqueducts, sometimes grooved into the side of a hill or straddling the backbone of a convenient ridge, it overcame formidable obstacles to connect the Hudson River with Lake Erie, and so provide the first practical link between East and West.

Such a great engineering work, even where long abandoned, could hardly fail to leave its impress across upper New York state. There remains of it, the truth must be said, little to rival the enduring monuments of imperial Rome, whose aqueducts, many times more ancient, still stand firm and strong, arch upon arch. The state of New York has been more prodigal of its relics, and the wrecker as well as time has demolished many of the old structures. But it is not easy to destroy a big ditch, and abundant traces of the old Erie remain.

That first Erie Canal was not quite the same one that extends across New York today. The original canal was twice enlarged and modernized, and each time considerable sections were rerouted. Many abandoned portions, forgotten and reclaimed by vines and brush, are still easily traceable across cornfields, or through orchards and thickets. But even today the attrition against these relics continues. David Plowden, while taking the photographs for this story, learned about an old basin—the canal equivalent of a harbor—where even the crumbling bones of several canal boats were to be seen. Although he set out at once with his equipment, he found a bulldozer grunting about where basin and boats had been only a day or two earlier. And where earth-moving machines have posed no threat to survivals of the canal, the public has sometimes taken the old ditch as an ideal depository for broken bed springs, beer cans, wrecked cars, and the other ephemera cast off by man as he aspires to the angels.

The old Erie well deserves to have something of it preserved. The Great Western Canal, it was called, and it was one of the prime highways of empire; this thin thread of water brought the western trade that made New York City into the great metropolis of the nation, and it was the way west that all but emptied entire New England hill towns.

The pre-eminence of the Erie Canal did not come about by happenstance. One of the hard realities with which the young American republic had to cope was that it was split fair in two by the Appalachian mountain range. Once a settler crossed that barrier he severed

The ERIE CANAL Passed This Way

Text by RALPH K. ANDRIST

Photographs by DAVID PLOWDEN

22

The traces of the old Erie Canal are not always obvious; the swatch of autumn foliage at upper left is rooted in a bit of dry and forgotten channel. Above is the side-cut lock at Watervliet, its gates long vanished, which permitted canal boats to cut through to the Hudson River in the background if they had no reason for remaining in the canal to Albany several miles farther on. Though the mood of the picture is one of serenity and isolation, the mottling on the water is detergent foam, and photographer David Plowden, making his pictures from a highway bridge, had as audience two boys stoning rats in a nearby dump. At left is the Hudson River entrance to the Erie Canal at Albany about 1825.

his old ties with the East completely—so completely that some people feared the trans-Appalachian West would form a separate nation. It was extremely difficult and prohibitively expensive to ship anything across the mountains; though an eastern market might be only two or three hundred miles away, a westerner found it cheaper and easier by far to ship by flatboat down to New Orleans, and then by sea around to the Atlantic coast, a matter of some three thousand miles.

From the St. Lawrence Valley until they dwindle away in Alabama, the Appalachians are broken in only one place: where the Hudson and Mohawk rivers flow through valleys carved by an ice-age torrent. This gap was an ancient Indian way, and then an early route of fur men, used and fought over by Dutch, French, English, and Americans. Fort Stanwix (later the site of Rome, New York) marked the strategic carrying place at the head of the Mohawk where travellers portaged their canoes two miles to Wood Creek, which took them into Oneida Lake, and thence on to the Oswego River and into Lake Ontario.

While this was a way through the mountains, it was by no means a smooth and easy route. Navigation on the Mohawk was completely barred near its mouth by Cohoes Falls. Navigation began at Schenectady, and some fifty-five miles west of that town another cataract, Little Falls, made a mile-long portage necessary. But on the river between, when the water was not too low, strong-backed boatmen could pole and haul craft known as Durham boats, forcing them through shallows and rapids and over stretches of sandbars. After the portage to Wood Creek there were more rapids and other hazards on the way down to Lake Ontario. And beyond that, for goods moving to or from the West, there was still transshipment around Niagara Falls. Yet, with all the necessary unloading and carrying and reloading, this was the only practical overland freight route to the West.

There were many half-formed plans for improving the waterway before 1792, when New York incorporated two private canal companies. The Northern Inland Lock Navigation Company began the next year to dig a canal from the Hudson River north to Lake Champlain, but it quickly went bankrupt. The Western Inland Lock Navigation Company also started work in 1793—its purpose being to improve the Mohawk River to the Lake Ontario waterway. In the next several years a canal was cut through the rocks around Little Falls, a mile more was dug to bypass another bad spot, and a channel and locks were completed connecting the Mohawk with Wood Creek. Durham boats as long as sixty feet and carrying sixteen tons of cargo were able to navigate the river in times of good water, where a ton and a half had been a good load

Although most of the abandoned sections of the old Erie Canal went dry, almost all of the stretch between Syracuse and Rome still serves as a feeder to carry water to the modern Barge Canal. At right is a quiet spot near Fayetteville on this part of the old canal; the towpath, pounded down by uncounted thousands of horse and mule hooves, is still clearly marked on the left bank. In contrast, the 1877 engraving of the canal below shows what it was like before trees and brush closed in. Above is a long-abandoned factory which was built on the old Erie when that canal was still a highroad of the Republic; the waterway here has become the broader Barge Canal, but the factory stares across it with empty windows, for a location on the canal is no longer the choice industrial site it once was.

before. The freight rates dropped correspondingly.

But the company found that a canal around Cohoes Falls was too much even to attempt, and goods still had to be transshipped from the Mohawk to the Hudson. Stockholders were called on again and again to pay extra assessments; dividends had been sporadic and usually small. The company finally expired in 1820 when its assets were purchased by the state of New York for the Erie Canal.

The difficulties of the Western Inland Lock Navigation Company did not dampen the enthusiasm or dim the bright visions of those who believed in the future of a practical waterway to the West. Credit for being the first to propose that a canal be dug all the long way from the Hudson River to Lake Erie, instead of only to Lake Ontario, is often given to Gouverneur Morris, statesman and patriot. In any event the idea, considered fantastic at first, gradually caught fire, and by 1808 a couple of upstate legislators arranged for a survey. The resulting report declared that the route to Lake Erie was superior to the shorter one to Lake Ontario.

By 1810 an Erie Canal was out of the dream stage. A board of commissioners was appointed to examine the possible routes. One of the seven members was De Witt Clinton, mayor of New York City, later to be governor, and henceforth to be inseparably linked with the Erie Canal. Another commissioner was Gouverneur Morris, broad of vision but impractical in his sweeping concepts. His pet scheme was an "incline plane," a waterway without locks, sloping gently downhill all the way from Lake Erie to the Hudson, six inches to the mile, flowing just enough to keep the channel always filled with water. As it turned out, the plan would have required excessive excavation and the building of high embankments to carry the canal over low places, and so was soon forgotten.

When the canal commission in its official report recommended a canal to Lake Erie rather than to Lake Ontario, the federal government was asked for help. When it refused, the state decided to go it alone. The War of 1812 intervened, but in March of 1817 the New York legislature at last approved the construction of an Erie Canal, but for the time being authorized only the digging of the middle section, from the upper Mohawk River near Rome to the Seneca River.

The canal was to be forty feet wide at the surface, sloping in to a bottom width of twenty-eight feet, and having a depth of four feet. Tentative plans had been drawn for the entire route from the Hudson to Lake Erie, but there would be much improvising as construction proceeded, to overcome unforeseen difficulties and to take advantage of the experience being acquired by the engineers. The completed canal, from the Hudson

26

Many of the abandoned locks of the bygone Erie Canal have been demolished because they stood in the way of a highway or other construction project, but none, so far as is known, has collapsed because of poor workmanship—the early masons built well. Below is a lock in Wayne County, its stonework still sound after many decades of neglect. Left: the grooves for the ironwork that once formed the pivot or hinge for one gate of the same lock are clearly visible in the stone. At right is a scene in Herkimer County in the 1850's; by then almost all locks had been doubled. Lockside stores allowed canalmen to shop while their boat waited to pass a lock.

History of Herkimer County (1879)

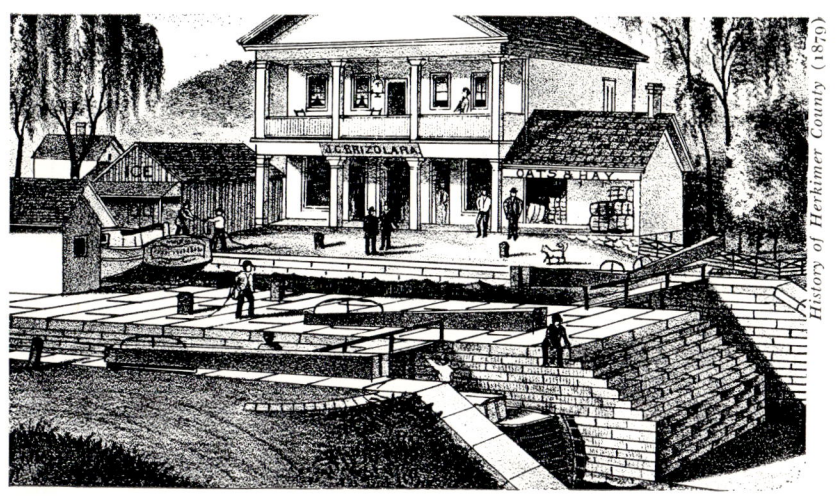

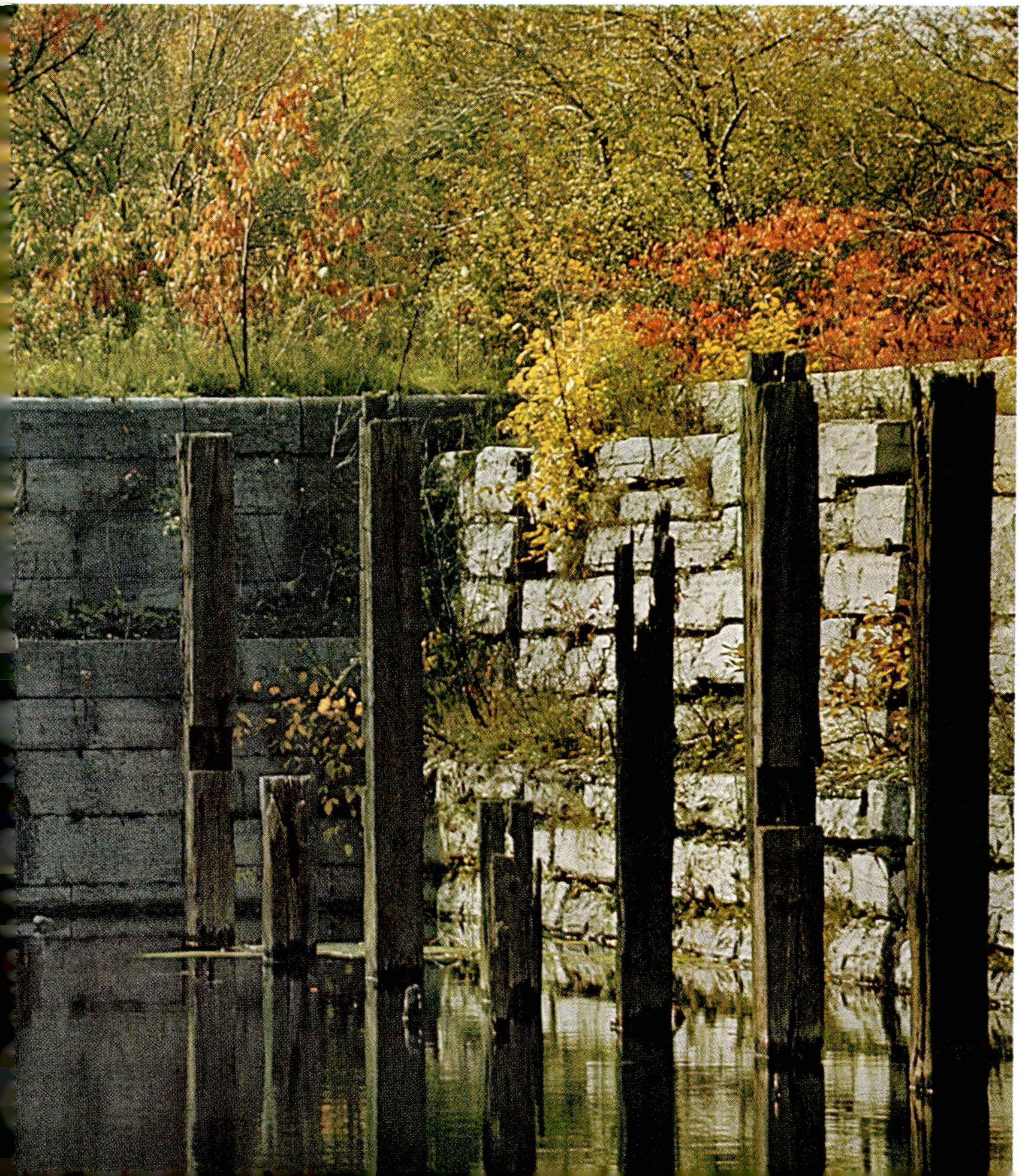

River to Lake Erie, would be 363 miles long. To overcome the 565-foot difference in level between river and lake (plus more than another hundred feet in steps up and down because of valleys) there would be eighty-four locks, each ninety feet long and fifteen feet wide. While the canal would cross many streams on its route at water level, it would bridge eighteen of them on aqueducts which would be engineering marvels of the time. All this the citizens of the state were to get at an estimated cost of less than five million dollars. At the same time, the legislators approved a canal from the Hudson River to Lake Champlain, for $871,000 more.

Construction started only a few months later; ground was broken on July 4, 1817, at Rome, at the head of the Mohawk. It was not for mere whim that the canal commissioners decided to start work in the middle of the route. In both eastern and western sections there would be much lock-building and extensive cutting through solid rock. But in the middle section the land was level, the soil deep and free of rocks. It was a good place to learn the art of canal building, about which no one really knew very much. The twenty-seven-mile Middlesex Canal between Boston and the Merrimack River was then by far the longest of the few American canals. There was no body of hydraulic engineering knowledge in the United States. Two of the Erie's chief engineers, Benjamin Wright and James Geddes, began work with experience limited largely to surveying. They and their colleagues would learn by doing.

The middle section was level, but it was not without its problems. It was largely forest land; much of the canal would have to be dug through huge stumps and roots. And supplies of all kinds had to be brought inland along the Mohawk by river and road. Nevertheless, the work went ahead. A sixty-foot path was staked out and cleared of trees and underbrush. Within this was another lane of stakes to mark the forty-foot width of the canal.

The digging was done by private contractors, often local farmers who improved their slack season by excavating a section of the ditch. Contracts were let for sections as short as a quarter of a mile. Within a year or so the use of axe and saw to cut down trees had given way to a quicker and easier method: one end of a cable was attached high on a tree and the other end to a roller turned by a crank and an endless screw arrangement. The crank and screw provided such tremendous mechanical advantage that one man could pull over a tree of almost any size. A stump-puller was devised which made use of the multiplied force provided by a huge wheel and axle. The materials for construction seemed to turn up when needed. Seepage of water threatened to be a serious problem when the first sections of canal were opened—but then a clay or

A canal aqueduct was simply a bridge that carried the waterway over a stream or valley, but it could be an imposing structure requiring a high degree of engineering skill, as these views of the Schoharie Creek aqueduct (above and at right) indicate. The towpath ran on top of the arched portion of the aqueduct; the timber flume or trough that carried the water was built between the arched section and the vertical stone piers, and rested at intervals on masonry supports. A clear idea of how it worked can be obtained by comparing the photographs with the woodcut at left, made about 1860, showing a boat being pulled across a similar canal aqueduct.

muck was found, called "the blue mud of the meadows," which proved an excellent seal when used as a liner. And a cement which hardened even under water took care of a very pressing need for a strong and lasting stonework mortar.

The first short section of canal was opened in the autumn of 1819, a little more than two years after construction had started. Water was turned into fifteen miles of channel between Rome and Utica, and a boat made the trip to Utica one day and back to Rome the next, towed by a team of horses and carrying a load of speechmaking dignitaries. Additional sections were put into service that same year, and by the next summer, 1820, the entire middle portion, ninety-four miles long, between Utica and Montezuma, carried water. As fast as sections were opened, boats appeared on them; even a part-way haul by water was better than none at all.

Digging on both the east and west sections then got under way, the crews working in both directions from the completed middle section, and each year new stretches were opened. In 1823 the Hudson River was reached, but it was 1825 before the western end cut through to Buffalo and Lake Erie. Almost overlooked in the excitement of these years was the completion of the Champlain Canal in 1823.

The Erie or "Great Western" Canal was sometimes called Clinton's Ditch. The nickname was coined in scorn by De Witt Clinton's political enemies—but, as is the fate of many pejoratives, it was soon adopted as a term of affection.

Bringing the canal along the Mohawk River had created special problems. In its lowest thirty miles, between Schenectady and Albany, the river was so squeezed between its rocky walls that at places the canal had to be cut into shelves above the water. And to complicate the difficulty, in this same stretch the river made its most precipitous plunge, so that twenty-seven of the eighty-four locks in the canal were in this short and cramped area. Here, too, was the Erie's longest aqueduct: at Crescent, only a dozen miles or so up the canal from Albany, the canal crossed from the south to the north side of the Mohawk on a "bridge" 1,188 feet long.

An Erie aqueduct was a specialized structure. Its masonry arches were designed to support a water-filled channel or flume of timber, which was, in fact, the canal itself. Usually the towpath on which the tow horses walked was an integral part of the masonry bridge rather than of the flume. The Crescent aqueduct was demolished many years ago, but twelve miles upstream at Alexander's Mills (now Rexford) the canal crossed back again to the south side of the river on another aqueduct. That aqueduct survived until

CONTINUED ON PAGE 77

On the earliest Erie Canal, locks were doubled for two-way traffic only at Lockport (right), where twin sets of five locks raised and lowered boats past a steep rock face. Today one of the sets of five has been replaced by two massive locks of the Barge Canal; the other set survives as a relic. Above are several of the venerable houses that line the canal at Lockport; below is an 1825 lithograph of the excavation of the waterway through solid rock west of Lockport, carved with powder and primitive tools.

CADWALLADER D. COLDEN, Memoir (1825)

30

It was almost election time, the unpopular war was stalemated, the casualty lists were growing, and the President's opponents cried "Peace!" Then the new commanding general moved with consummate political as well as military skill

GRANT *and the* POLITICIANS

By BRUCE CATTON

In a notable dispatch sent to Abraham Lincoln on May 11, 1864, General Ulysses S. Grant, who was then waist-deep in the fearful battle of Spotsylvania Court House, promised that he would "fight it out on this line if it takes all summer." All summer it did take, and all fall and all winter as well, and although victory finally came, it looked for a while as if Grant's road to military success would lead straight to a disastrous political failure; one of those who thought so being President Abraham Lincoln. A few years later, when Grant himself had spent some time in the White House, it seemed that U. S. Grant could be written off as a tenacious but unimaginative soldier who had no political comprehension whatever and who as a result may have cost more than democracy could afford.

This verdict has been more or less current ever since; which is too bad, because it is entirely wrong.

To see that it is wrong one need do no more than take a fresh look at 1864, when General Grant showed a political awareness and sensitivity such as few American soldiers have ever shown. If he had not done so, the Union cause would almost certainly have failed, once and for all, before the end of the year. For the essence of Grant's problem that summer was that he had to make it politically possible for the military victory to be won. He knew that in the end Federal might would wear down and crush the southern Confederacy, provided that the people of the North were willing to go on applying it. To maintain their will at the necessary intensity was of course Lincoln's responsibility, but Lincoln would not be around to discharge that responsibility unless Grant played the political caroms intelligently.

To put it more simply: Grant had to make certain that the intense Federal war effort did not defeat Lincoln before it defeated Robert E. Lee.

As the month of July ended, the military situation was static, unsatisfactory, and infernally beset by political complications.

Lee and his great Army of Northern Virginia were pinned down at Petersburg, Virginia, an extensively fortified town on the Appomattox River which in effect constituted the defense of Richmond. Facing Lee, Grant had George G. Meade's Army of the Potomac and Benjamin Butler's Army of the James; their armies were so strong that Lee could not get away but not strong enough so that they themselves could get into the Confederate capital. For the moment, the war here was a standoff.

It looked like a standoff in Georgia as well, where William Tecumseh Sherman sought to get into Atlanta while Confederate General John B. Hood tried to drive him away. The situation here was much like that at Richmond, except that Hood was about to make the

---

In war the important thing, noted Winston Churchill, is resolution; and it is equally true that the lack of it can be disastrous. We have seen both sides of this homely truth displayed in modern times, one way in World War II, another at the Bay of Pigs. As this goes to the printer, America has not yet made up its mind about another case, in Vietnam. Once upon a time, over a century ago, it faced the same issue, in the late, agonizing stages of the Civil War. What happened then is described most penetratingly in this abridgement of portions from Grant Takes Command, *by Bruce Catton, which will be published early next year by Little, Brown and Company.*—The Editors

33

enormous mistake of trying to take the offensive—a game which he could not hope to win, although he did not yet realize it. Farther west the rival forces were not really at grips. What happened in Virginia and Georgia would finally settle what happened beyond the Mississippi and along the Gulf coast.

The most sensitive point at the moment was the upper end of the Shenandoah Valley and the Potomac country around Harpers Ferry and Martinsburg. Here Lee had a small but active army led by the energetic Jubal Early, who was not strong enough to invade the north but was altogether too strong to be ignored. The Federal government had massed a large number of soldiers at Washington—including thousands who were badly needed at Petersburg—but had been unable to make Early retreat.

As far as the average northerner could see, things were going badly. Neither of the chief Confederate strongholds, Richmond and Atlanta, had fallen or seemed likely to fall; Federal casualty lists in Virginia had been appalling and apparently had been wasted; Early was threatening Washington, it seemed, just about as much as Grant was threatening Richmond, and the war was beginning to look like an outright failure. Furthermore—and this was the crucial point—the country was about to elect a President. Nobody before had ever tried to do this in the middle of a civil war, but it was going to be tried now because the nation's ability to do it was somehow, under everything else, what the war was all about. There was a strong peace party, and an even stronger party that wanted reunion but would accept slavery in order to get it, and if between them these groups named the next President, the war would almost certainly be lost.

Grant understood this, and he wanted to win the victories that would ensure Lincoln's re-election. But he saw, too, that if the political price for these victories was too high Lincoln might lose. A case in point was Grant's recent attempt to shelve General Butler, who was a military incompetent. He had been unable to do it because Butler had political power which the administration simply dared not alienate. Similarly, politics kept Grant from naming General William Franklin to the top command of the fragmented levies that were trying without success to defeat General Early. In the same way, it was not possible to touch the command structure of the Army of the Potomac without sending political tremors all across Washington.

The whole problem came to a head on July 31, when Grant and Lincoln had a face-to-face, unpublicized meeting at Fort Monroe. The meeting was called to discuss Grant's desire to get a good commander for the campaign against Early, but it ranged on and gave Grant a full picture of the claims of politics in a presidential year.

Neither Lincoln nor Grant ever said much about the meeting, but what took place is fairly clear. On July 30 Grant had telegraphed to the President, promising to meet him at Fort Monroe the next day, and on the back of this telegram Lincoln scribbled a few words that could only be a listing of the points to be discussed: "Meade & Franklin / McClellan / Md & Penna."

The "Meade & Franklin" bit came first. Lincoln apparently told Grant what Grant already knew: he could not have Franklin. Then he went on to Meade, asking Grant whether Meade would be willing to leave the Army of the Potomac and take command of the forces opposing General Early. Grant had mentioned this to Meade a few days earlier and had received no reply except the remark that Meade was "ready to obey any order that might be given me." Actually, Meade rather liked the idea; he had told his wife that "so far as having an independent command, which the Army of the Potomac is not, I would like this change very well," although he confessed that the notion of taking charge of all the different generals who held forth in the Washington area and dealing directly with Secretary of War Edwin Stanton and the Chief of Staff, General Henry Halleck, was somewhat sobering. In any case, the President pointed out that in recent months there had been a good deal of agitation for Meade's dismissal, and if the transfer were made now it would look as if the President had given way under pressure. However all of this may have been, Grant after this chat with Lincoln gave no more thought to the plan for sending Meade to the Potomac.

That Lincoln included a "Md & Penna" item is not surprising. He understood the need for a unified command and was ready to go along with it, the only question being the choice of the man to hold that command. It is here that his jotted "McClellan" becomes of interest. A note in General Marsena Patrick's catchall diary of headquarters understandings provides a clue. Shortly after this meeting, Patrick wrote: "The same proposition of consolidation was urged in behalf of [General George B.] McClellan by very strong Republicans for two reasons. One, that by giving him military position it would dispose of him politically—the other, that his name would bring forward a host of volunteers." Patrick added that "the plan was rejected at Washington," but either the rejection had not yet been made final, or some of Lincoln's official family had not got the word. More was going on here than Patrick realized.

The Democrats were to hold their convention at the end of August in Chicago, and it was generally assumed that McClellan was going to be the nominee. Various Republican leaders wanted to head this off; in May, Postmaster General Montgomery Blair had begun writing letters to the New York financier and Democratic party notable, S. L. M. Barlow, who was close to McClellan. In these letters Blair had suggested a clever deal: let the Democrats and moderate Republicans make common cause against the Republican Radicals and unite behind Lincoln, with McClellan removing himself from the political race and accepting for recompense a high command in the army. This would ensure Lincoln's reelection and would also be good for McClellan: "He is young, and there is a great future opening to one of his genius and antecedents"—and, in fine, he could run for the Presidency after the war was over and Lincoln had finished his second term.

Barlow said that Thurlow Weed, Republican leader in New York, had made the same suggestion to him, and later in the summer he told McClellan that reliable sources said Lincoln was looking for Democratic support, offering to put McClellan back in high command in return. On July 20—less than two weeks before Lincoln and Grant had their meeting—one of Barlow's informants reported that Blair's father, Francis P. Blair, Sr., was in New York, trying to get an appointment with McClellan. This appointment Blair presently got, and he urged McClellan to apply for a military assignment, remarking that if Lincoln refused to give it to him "he would then be responsible for the consequences." McClellan gave him a noncommittal answer, and if the plan interested him he never did anything about it. Presumably he thought it best to go ahead with the political race, especially since the war was going badly and a useful political issue was the fact that McClellan was not being used. (Barlow had wondered if anyone "will forgive Mr. Lincoln for the monstrous crime of permitting the great fight of the war to take place without the benefit of his personality.")

CONTINUED ON PAGE 81

This pro-Lincoln cartoon recalls the passions of the 1864 presidential campaign. Lincoln is supported by three stalwarts: Republican Senator Charles Sumner of Massachusetts, chairman of the Foreign Relations Committee; Grant; and Rear Admiral David Farragut, the hero of Mobile Bay. By contrast, the Democratic candidate, General George B. McClellan, is assisted toward his cheesy platform by Peace Democrats Clement L. Vallandigham of Ohio and two New Yorkers, Governor Horatio Seymour and Fernando Wood, former mayor of New York City. The three ordinary citizens in the middle are evidently Irish immigrants, whom upper-class Republicans of the time looked upon as the dregs of society.

GALVESTON, SEPTEMBER 8, 1900:

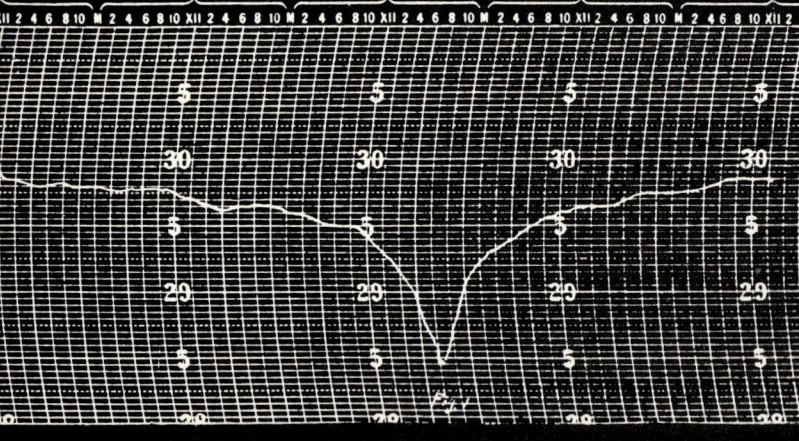

WHEN THE HURRICANE STRUCK

By JOHN E. WEEMS

Weatherman Joseph L. Cline worked late in the austere quarters of the Galveston office Friday night, September 7, 1900. A twenty-nine-year-old bachelor, a nondrinker in a city where liquor flowed, and a man who was fascinated by his work, Cline did not object to the hours. Furthermore, his own brother Isaac was in charge of the office and had helped him get the job; Isaac was, he reasoned, entitled to loyalty.

Still, Joseph Cline was weary, and he was looking forward to sleep. In addition to handling his usual duties that day, he and his brother and a third observer, John D. Blagden, had become increasingly concerned about a tropical cyclone whirling somewhere to the southeast, over the tepid Gulf of Mexico.

The storm had first been reported to Galveston on Tuesday, the fourth, when the Weather Bureau's central office in Washington, D.C., sent a terse wire: "Tropical storm disturbance moving northward over Cuba." In those days only the central office had authority to issue storm warnings; about all anyone else could do was watch the weather, telegraph his own observations, wait for central office advisories, and distribute them when the time came.

But it had seemed, for this disturbance, that the time would not come. On Tuesday the storm had rolled across Cuba and was travelling almost due north, apparently heading for Florida. On the following morning its center was a short distance northwest of Key West. On Thursday, however, the storm had veered almost due west, and by Friday the center was somewhere southeast of the Louisiana coast.

At 10:30 that morning Isaac Cline had received notification that Galveston should be included in the storm warning. Five minutes later he ran two signal pennants up the pole atop the Levy Building, where the Weather Bureau was located. They flapped in a seventeen-mile-

ROSENBERG LIBRARY, GALVESTON

per-hour wind. Most Galvestonians knew that the red flag with a black center meant that a storm of "marked violence" was expected. Above that flag fluttered a white pennant: the storm would come from the northwest. Since winds of a tropical cyclone blow counterclockwise around a relatively calm center, or eye, the central office had thus evidently forecast that the hurricane would move inland somewhere east of Galveston. Isaac reflected that if this happened the city would be in less danger, studies having shown that cyclone damage was less on the left side than on the right, where the speed of the storm's advance is added to the storm's wind velocity.

That Friday morning the Galveston weathermen had noticed the first clear signs of an approaching hurricane: an increasing Gulf swell, rolling in from the southeast, and feathery cirrus clouds. The cirrus, too, came from the southeast; there were only a few at first, but a trained observer would know that they presaged heavier clouds.

During the day, Joseph had become aware of this tropical storm, but his increasing anxiety was not much more than a weatherman's usual concern for contributing to an accurate forecast—for providing advance notice of a weather change.

Neither were other Galvestonians especially worried. Theirs was, after all, a substantial city: with 37,000 inhabitants, it was the fourth largest in Texas—a flourishing commercial center, a tourist attraction, a seat of culture. Moreover, the residents of this island municipality had become familiar with tropical hurricanes; Galveston had survived many in the past. First floors of residences and business buildings were elevated several feet above the sandy ground level as a safeguard against "overflows," tidal inundations of the city. An overflow was frequently an occasion for a holiday—clerks went home and youngsters splashed in the streets. The atmosphere was like that in a northern city during a snowstorm.

As the storm edged closer late that Friday night, Joseph completed his day's duties. Working by the light of a bare electric bulb, he finished a weather map, the only task now keeping him from sleep. Then he left the building and walked through empty, breeze-cooled streets to the post office, where he deposited the map for dispatch on an early-morning train to the Texas interior. Roused somewhat by the exertion, he then hiked more than a mile to his brother's home, four blocks from the beach, where he had a room. At one o'clock he sank into bed; his sleep was restless despite his weariness.

Isaac Cline's sturdy, two-story frame house was situated on a lot that was 5.2 feet above sea level. It had been built to withstand Gulf storms—to withstand the worst storm, in fact, that its owner could imagine, and he had been in the weather service eighteen years, eleven of them in Galveston. The first floor was elevated above the high-water mark of Galveston's most recent big overflow, a storm in 1875 that had brought with it an 8.2-foot tide.

The house reflected the Cline brothers' methodical personalities. Both were practical, serious, rather scholarly men of remarkable integrity. Both had earned Ph.D.'s from AddRan College, now Texas Christian University in Fort Worth. Both were tall, slim, active; they prided themselves on their good health, which they guarded carefully. Isaac and his wife, Cora May, had three daughters, aged twelve, eleven, and six.

While Joseph slept, the morning edition of the Galveston *News* was being printed. In it appeared a local weather story whose hopeful final paragraph noted that at midnight "the moon was shining brightly and the sky was not as threatening as earlier in the night. The weather bureau had no late advices as to the storm's movements and it may be that the tropical disturbance has changed its course or spent its force. . . ."

But anyone who had observed the tide now thunder-

The Galveston hurricane, with its estimated six to eight thousand victims, was the worst recorded natural disaster ever to hit the North American continent. By 8 P.M. on September 8, 1900, the barometric pressure had fallen to 28.48 inches—at that point a record low reading for the United States Weather Bureau. In the wake of the storm: a child's hand, left, frozen in death; a fire wagon—one of many—carting bodies to barges, above, for burial at sea (some corpses, underweighted, drifted back ashore); and two well-dressed survivors.

ing ashore to the south would have known the storm had not changed course. The swells had increased continuously, and they were rolling ever farther inland against a stiffening north wind that ordinarily would have tended to break them up.

Four blocks from the beach, in the room where Joseph slept, the roar of the breakers was audible; perhaps that explained why he slept so fitfully. At four o'clock he awoke, filled with what he later described as a "sense of impending disaster."

"I sensed," he said, "that the waters of the Gulf were already over our back yard. One glance out of the south window . . . showed me that my presentiment was correct. I immediately awoke my brother."

The two Clines decided on a division of duties: Joseph would return to the office to handle observations and to telegraph developments to the central office. Isaac would harness the horse to his two-wheeled cart and hurry to the beach to awaken residents and warn them back to higher ground. He was to keep an eye on the rising tide.

Before five o'clock, then, Isaac stood watching the dirty brown turbulence that was the Gulf—where only a few days earlier there had been crowds of tourists from all over the state enjoying late-summer relaxation in the clean sand and warm surf. He observed the swells, and the wind blowing ineffectually against them, and he drafted a message for the central office: "Unusually heavy swells from the southeast, intervals one to five minutes, overflowing low places south portion of city three to four blocks from beach. Such high water with opposing winds never observed previously." Cline knew this was no ordinary storm tide.

Immediately he began a Revere-like ride up and down the beach, warning people to leave low areas. Comparatively few heeded his advice. Most residents, having experienced overflows before, were not worried. They were

CONTINUED ON PAGE 74

39

HISTORY AT MIDDLE DISTANCE

The charge was rape. The accuser was a southern white woman, the accused were Negroes. But what kind of woman was Victoria Price? And what had really happened aboard that freight train?

A Reasonable Doubt

BY DAN T. CARTER

The Scottsboro Case—an infamous series of litigations which was to inflame both the North and the South for many years—began inconspicuously on March 25, 1931, as white and Negro hobos brawled aboard a freight train moving across northeastern Alabama. One of the white youths thrown from the train reported the fight to the nearest stationmaster, and a Jackson County posse stopped the train at the rural village of Paint Rock. When deputies removed the nine Negro teenagers on board they also discovered two young white girls, aged seventeen and twenty-one, who were hitching a ride from Chattanooga, Tennessee, back to their home in Huntsville, Alabama. In the first confusing minutes after the arrests, Ruby Bates whispered to officials that she and her friend, Victoria Price, had been raped by the nine Negroes, who ranged in age from twelve to nineteen. A hasty medical examination revealed evidence of sexual intercourse.

That night, sheriff's deputies, strengthened by the Alabama National Guard, averted a mass lynching after a sullen mob gathered outside the Jackson County jailhouse in the little town of Scottsboro. Two weeks later, while a crowd of eight to ten thousand filled Scottsboro's streets, two court-appointed attorneys half-heartedly defended the frightened boys. Four juries convicted and sentenced eight to death; the trial of Leroy Wright, aged twelve, for whom the state had asked a life sentence, ended in a hung jury.

Cases similar to the Scottsboro one had been largely unnoticed outside the South. But the number of defendants, their extreme youth, the stunning rapidity of the trials, and the harsh sentences the boys received attracted the attention of national newspapers. In April, the International Labor Defense, a close affiliate of the Communist party, launched a propaganda campaign to expose what it called "the Alabama frame-up." Although the N.A.A.C.P. belatedly offered legal support to the convicted youths, the I.L.D. swiftly gained the backing of the boys and their parents. In late December of 1931, N.A.A.C.P. attorneys withdrew from the case.

The United States Supreme Court accepted the I.L.D.'s contention that the youths had had inadequate legal counsel at Scottsboro and overturned the convictions in 1932. But the rallies, pamphlets, and flamboyant accusations of the International Labor Defense and the Communist party only stiffened the resolve of Alabamians to repel the accusations of "outsiders" and see the Scottsboro defendants put to death. As the new trials approached in the spring of 1933, the International Labor Defense reluctantly turned to one of the nation's most brilliant criminal attorneys, Samuel S. Leibowitz of Brooklyn, New York. Leibowitz did not subscribe to the I.L.D. ideology, but he felt that the boys' basic civil rights had been violated, and when the I.L.D.'s executive secretary promised to shelve temporarily his organization's revolutionary rhetoric, Leibowitz agreed to defend the youths without fee.

He began the case with a plea for a change of venue, and the presiding judge agreed to transfer the trials fifty miles west of Scottsboro to Decatur, the seat of Morgan County. There, with a National Guard unit on duty to keep order, the second series of trials began in late March. The first defendant to be tried was Haywood Patterson, nineteen.

March 27, the opening day, was warm and clear in Decatur. Before 7 A.M. a large and cheerful crowd had gathered outside the two-story yellow brick courthouse. Even the announcement that there would be a half-day's delay in the proceedings did not seem to dispel the spectators' good nature. Throughout the morning they sunned lazily on the wide lawn or gossiped around the two courthouse statues, one honoring justice and the other paying tribute to those Confederate soldiers "who gave their lives for a just cause—State's Rights." There was some talk about the trial, but mostly the relaxed crowd discussed the Depression. Three and a half years after the crash of 1929, these Alabamians—like most Americans—were optimistically looking to Mr. Roosevelt and his New Deal for relief. For as the cotton mills and railroad shops had closed or curtailed their operations, hard times had come to Decatur. The spring foliage and flowers camouflaged, but they could not conceal, the empty, dilapidated stores downtown and the peeling paint on the outlying houses.

Samuel Leibowitz had been apprehensive when he first arrived in Decatur. He was keenly aware that he and his fellow defense attorney, Joseph Brodsky, were outsiders. Worse, they were New York Jews. To his relief, however, the townspeople greeted him with unaffected hospitality. "[They] . . . impress me as being honest, God-fearing people who want to see justice done," he told reporters.

After lunch, as officials announced that the court would soon convene, an irregular line formed, stretching through the courthouse corridors and past the brass spittoons resting on their tobacco-stained rubber pads. Within minutes, the 425 seats were filled—whites in three sections, Negroes in the fourth. At 2 P.M., Judge James Edwin Horton, Jr., settled into the raised judge's chair, adjusted his tortoise-shell spectacles, and nodded to the prosecutor to begin reading the indictment.

Lank, raw-boned and more than six feet tall, Horton strongly resembled photographs of the young and beardless Lincoln. His family had served prominently in the political life of the ante-bellum South, and the fifty-five-year-old judge spoke without self-consciousness of his obligation to uphold the integrity of the family name. His views on the Negro, like those of the traditionally conservative southerner, were kindly and well-meaning, with a trace of *noblesse oblige*, yet when one of the two Negro reporters present introduced himself on the first day of the trial, Horton, in the presence of disapproving townspeople, unhesitatingly offered a firm handshake. In the Decatur courtroom he was easygoing and lenient, unbothered by the clatter of reporters' noisy typewriters. During the two-week trial he had to rule upon many questions of law that he had accepted without question throughout his legal career; generally he remained calm

BOTH: BROWN BROTHERS

Flanked by National Guardsmen, the nine "Scottsboro boys" pose with defense attorney Samuel Leibowitz in a narrow prison corridor. Seated on a box at the lawyer's left is Haywood Patterson.

and unruffled, his voice at an even, conversational level.

To the disappointment of the spectators, the sensational testimony that they expected to hear did not begin right away. In fact, the whole first week of the trial was taken up with a complex constitutional duel between defense and state attorneys over the question of Negro jurors, and the crowd quickly lost interest. Leibowitz argued that Alabama officials had defied the Fourteenth Amendment by excluding Negroes from the Jackson County juries which had originally convicted the nine youths, and from the Morgan County venire from which a new jury would now be chosen to retry the first defendant, Haywood Patterson. The absence of Negro jurors was incontestable; a courtroom official said he could not recall seeing black men in the jury box since before the turn of the century. But a Scottsboro civic leader explained on the witness stand that the absence of Negro jurors was not a matter of racial prejudice. It was simply that Negroes had not been "trained for jury duty in our county . . . and I don't think their judgment—you could depend on it altogether." Besides, he added as the spectators chuckled, "they will nearly all steal." One jury commissioner told Leibowitz that Negroes were not excluded for any particular reason; "Negroes was never discussed."

Thomas Knight, Jr., Alabama's thirty-four-year-old attorney general, was present to handle the prosecution. Affable and charming, he ordinarily conveyed the image of well-bred southern gentility. In the courtroom, however, he was a fierce antagonist. Nervously pacing across the courtroom, he alternately cajoled and threatened the apprehensive Negro leaders from Scottsboro and Decatur who testified on the jury question. The nineteen witnesses included a Pullman porter, the owner of a dry-cleaning shop, a dentist, a seminary-trained minister, and a doctor educated at Phillips Exeter Academy in New Hampshire and the University of Illinois. Knight succeeded in showing that some of them were unaware of the intricate details of the jury selection system and that others did not know all the legal requirements for jury duty. He was not able to conceal, however, what Leibowitz wanted to prove: that the Negro witnesses were completely qualified to serve as jurors yet that, because of their race, none had ever been called.

"The vaginal examination showed . . . [the spermatozoa] were nonmotile."
—Dr. R. R. Bridges

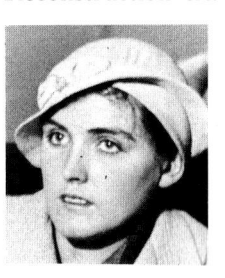

"I told it just like Victoria Price told it."
—Surprise witness Ruby Bates

"My God, Doctor, is this whole thing a horrible mistake?"
—Judge James Horton

After four days of testimony and argument, Horton denied Leibowitz's motions to quash the Jackson County indictment and set aside the Morgan County venire. Significantly, however, he also ruled that the jury rolls of both counties contained only the names of whites. A smiling Leibowitz perfunctorily objected to the court's decision; privately he told friends he was confident no conviction could now withstand the scrutiny of the United States Supreme Court.

Despite Leibowitz's pleasure at the progress of the trial, reporters had sensed a shift of local mood from geniality to distrust and then to anger. However well-intentioned Morgan County citizens might be, their ultimate loyalty was to preserving the racial status quo. Still buried in the walls of several of the town's buildings were bullets fired during the Civil War; the entire area had been a center of Ku Klux Klan strength during the Reconstruction era and again in the Klan resurgence of the 1920's. Leibowitz's insistence on referring to Negro witnesses as "Mr." had perplexed the spectators, but when he pressed his demand for Negro jurors, grim hostility appeared on the faces of the overalled farmers. Leibowitz, warned a Black Belt newspaper, had "thrown down the challenge to . . . white supremacy."

Judge Horton's brief remarks to the venire of jurors on Friday afternoon referred obliquely to the rising hostility. "Now, gentlemen," he said, "under our law when it comes to the courts we know neither black nor white. . . . It is our duty to mete out even-handed justice. . . . No other course is open to you"—his voice suddenly became stern and harsh—"and let no one think they can act otherwise." The judge's implicit warning ended the open threats which had been heard on Decatur's streets, but resentment smouldered beneath the surface, a resentment bolstered by the presence of "outside radicals" who had come to observe the proceedings.

The jury was selected in one afternoon. Leibowitz was not altogether satisfied, since the state had used its challenges to exclude younger men who might have had "liberal" ideas, but at least he felt he had managed to keep the most obvious "red-neck" types off the jury.

When the actual taking of testimony began the following Monday, the seats were jammed for the first time since the opening day. Although it was cool in the building when the courtroom doors opened at 8:30 A.M., within an hour the spectators had begun to shed their

"I hung my hat on a little limb and went to having intercourse with the girl."
—Defense witness Lester Carter

coats, and by noon courthouse officials were forced to turn on the overhead fans to dispel the oppressive stuffiness caused by constant smoking in the crowded courtroom. Just before 9 A.M. Victoria Price, the older of the two complainants, took the stand. (The other girl, Ruby Bates, was absent; although she had testified at the trials two years before in Scottsboro, state officials said that she had recently disappeared.) Mrs. Price wore a blue straw hat and a black dress with a fichu of white lace at the throat. Her stylish costume was quite unlike the bedraggled outfit she had worn at Scottsboro, and in keeping with her new mien, she restrained her habit of chewing snuff, which at earlier hearings had necessitated frequent spitting. She seemed nervous in the witness chair, crossing and uncrossing her legs and fingering her long necklace of glass beads. When Attorney General Knight began his questioning, however, she spoke in a clear, firm voice that carried to the back of the courtroom.

Mrs. Price began her story from the time she and her friend Ruby boarded the train at Chattanooga to return to their home in Huntsville. Just south of Stevenson, Alabama, she said, about a dozen Negro youths leaped from the top of an adjacent boxcar into the gondola that she and Ruby were sharing with seven white hobos. After a brief scuffle, all but one of the outnumbered white boys were thrown from the train. The only remaining white, Orville Gilley, was forced to watch the brutal assaults that followed. Thrusting her finger toward Haywood Patterson, Mrs. Price identified him as one of the rapists. Knight asked her if Patterson's "private parts penetrated your private parts." "Yes sir, they did," she replied. Suddenly Knight pulled a torn cotton undergarment from his briefcase, and asked Victoria Price to state whether these were the step-ins she was wearing at the time of the assault. Leibowitz leaped to his feet. "This is the first time in two years any such step-ins have ever been shown" in connection with the case, he objected. "They are here now," Knight answered, grinning, and tossed them into the lap of one of the bewildered jurors. The courtroom exploded into laughter, and Judge Horton had to gavel for quiet. In less than twenty minutes the Alabama attorney general completed his direct examination and, with a gracious smile toward the defense table, abandoned his star witness to Leibowitz.

The balding lawyer, younger than most spectators had anticipated, exuded confidence. During his career he had reduced even honest witnesses to incoherent confusion, and he was convinced that Victoria Price was lying. Leibowitz had all the skills of a good trial lawyer: an actor's sense of timing, a flair for the dramatic, and a clear, forceful voice. But his main strength was an almost infallible memory for detail and, above all, for contradictions. "I am not a great lawyer," he had once said in response to a compliment. "I'm only thorough." He began his cross-examination gently, almost kindly: "Miss Price . . . shall I call you Miss Price or Mrs. Price?" "Mrs. Price," answered the witness sullenly. She looked at her interrogator as though he were a poisonous snake circling her chair.

For more than three hours Leibowitz put her through a grueling cross-examination. First, he sought to discredit her testimony by proving she was a known prostitute and thus unworthy of belief. Second, by confusing her in cross-examination he hoped to convince the jury that she was lying. Finally, he planned to reveal what had really happened during the forty-eight hours preceding the alleged assault.

It was easy enough to discredit Mrs. Price's claim to be a "southern lady." In Huntsville, with the nickname of Big Leg Price, she was a well-known streetwalker. Leibowitz introduced arrest and conviction records showing she had been found guilty of "adultery and fornication" on January 26, 1931, with a Huntsville married man, L. J. "Jack" Tiller. But Mrs. Price proved unexpectedly difficult to entangle in cross-examination. Using a model of the freight train, Leibowitz tried to illustrate the sequence of events. Mrs. Price adamantly refused to agree that the model looked like the train she had ridden. What were the differences? asked Leibowitz. "That is not the train I was on," she snapped. "It was bigger, lots bigger, that is a toy." No amount of cajoling from Leibowitz could force from her an admission that it was a suitable replica.

During the trials in Scottsboro, Mrs. Price had been colorful and inventive in her account of the assault. At

"If you acquit this Negro, put a garland of roses around his neck . . ."
—Prosecutor Thomas Knight, Jr.

"What [the prosecution] is saying is 'Come on, boys! We can lick this Jew from New York!'"
—Defense attorney Samuel Leibowitz

CONTINUED ON PAGE 95

Can it be recaptured? I wondered as the Verdun train rocked south through the darkened farmlands of Champagne. Can another generation really grasp this old lost thing that you have held and heard in imagination and in long night talks? *Have another drink. The whiz-bangs were the worst....* The solid men with the beefy, cheerful faces, those big hands like stones on the red Formica table top. *I remember the first time I went into the lines....* Can it be recaptured, that already ancient time, shadowed by the racing madness of another war, those days and nights you heard about so often?

The Argonne....

The greatest battle in American history. That is what they called it in the twenties, and even today, in terms of mass, concentration, and carnage, it still deserves the title. A million and a quarter Americans, jammed into a fighting front little more than twenty miles wide and forty miles deep. But it is not history you are riding toward now. It is memory, it is part of the large pulse that still beats deep in your body at the word *father*. You hope, this once, to write a different kind of history, a personal, perhaps impossible thing. You want nothing less than to recapture him—and all the rest of them, those puttee-clad doughboys with upside-down tin dishes on their heads, the Americans of 1918 who marched, singing, into the Argonne.

There was no generation gap between my father and me. He treated me like a man from the age of fifteen. I went with him to political dinners and veterans' reunions, spent innumerable midnights sitting up with him and his friends in our Jersey City kitchen while my poor mother remonstrated feebly from the upper floor. My ears always grew sharp when the talk turned, as it inevitably did, to the war. The stories would spill out, almost always funny but sometimes brutal. About cooties, the lice that made sweaters walk. About three days in the lines eating nothing but carrots. About the nervous sentry who bayoneted his own pack in the dark. About the shell that plowed into the mud a foot away from a private, who dug it out and found he and it had the same serial number. About the Garden of Allah, the first French whorehouse they found when they got off the boat at Calais. About the air attacks a few hours after they debarked, and the enraged few who slung hand grenades into a German prisoner-of-war compound to revenge their wounded buddies. About Harry Ross, the company screwball, who marched an entire platoon onto a Paris train, without a leave pass among them.

My father had been a sergeant in the 78th Division, and most of his fellow Jerseymen had soldiered with the

An Army Signal Corps photographer dramatically captured the mood of the

Half a century later, an American writer in France tries to recapture the unforgettable experience of his father in the greatest battle fought by the doughboys "over there"

T*wo*

44

fighting in the Meuse-Argonne in this snapshot taken on October 11, 1918.

Argonnes

By THOMAS J. FLEMING

Lt. Thomas J. "Teddy" Fleming, the father of the author, in 1918

same outfit. Almost all the World War I divisions were organized along state or sectional lines. The 78th was at first called "the President's Own" division, because Woodrow Wilson had been New Jersey's governor. Later the men voted to call it the "Lightning" division, in honor of the famed Jersey brew surreptitiously distilled in the pine woods around Fort Dix.

Inevitably, once past these preliminaries, the reminiscing turned to the Western Front. I listened hypnotically to names that meant nothing to me. St.-Mihiel, Thiaucourt, the "Limey Sector," Argonne, the Bois des Loges, Grandpré, Talma, Bellejoyeuse Farm. But it was all discussed in a peculiarly unheroic way. There was never a trace of braggadocio in the battle stories. Only from others did I discover that Sergeant Fleming had been made an acting lieutenant in the Argonne. Only when I asked to see them did he show me his meticulous notes on infantry tactics, the huge black .45-caliber automatic he had brought home, the division's battle maps filled with those French names that rolled so readily (if inaccurately) off the tongues of all veterans.

At the same time, my knowledge of the battle remained curiously vague. I had the standard American impression that the Argonne was a vast forest through which the Yanks had swarmed tumultuously to defeat the Germans in the decisive battle of the war. When I began planning my trip to France a few months ago, my father had been dead almost ten years. I realized I did not even know his regiment or company. A visit to the forty-ninth reunion of the 78th Division at Fort Dix cleared up these minor mysteries. "Teddy" Fleming, or "Red" as some of the old veterans called him, had been a sergeant in Company C of the 312th Regiment.

Otherwise the reunion was a sad and somewhat frustrating experience. All my father's close friends were dead. In discussing the Argonne, the surviving old soldiers were unbelievably vague about details. Like my father and his friends, they preferred the funny memories—stealing chickens, chasing French girls, outwitting second lieutenants or MP's. It made me realize, with something of a shock, how little death or wounds, fatigue or hunger, fear or bravery, had been mentioned in the stories I had heard when my father was alive. The commanding officer of the contemporary 78th Division, Major General John G. Cassidy, slashed all sorts of red tape to give me access to company and regimental histories. But I left Fort Dix with little more than the raw material of personal history. It was clear that if I was going to recapture my father's Argonne, much would depend on what the place itself gave me.

TEXT CONTINUED ON PAGE 48
MEUSE-ARGONNE MAP OVERLEAF

The Doughboys' Greatest Battle

The Meuse-Argonne offensive was the greatest battle American soldiers fought in the First World War—the greatest battle the American Army had ever fought up to that time, which was the fall of 1918. The battle was over twenty-five miles wide and thirty-five miles deep, it went on from September 26 to November 11, from first to last it involved something like 1,250,000 American soldiers, and as long as military history is written or remembered it will be recalled as one of the greatest and most costly of American military achievements.

The Meuse-Argonne was part of the enormous Allied blow that broke the back of the Imperial German Army and brought the war to an end. On the left of the Americans the French were driving forward; beyond the French, the British were smashing across northern France in a great all-out effort. Outnumbered, and led by a high command that had lost its morale and its grip on the situation, the German soldiers were putting up a game but losing battle. Allied victory was obviously somewhere ahead, but there was a great deal of hard fighting to be done before it could be won. In the Meuse-Argonne, the Americans got their full share of it.

The final objective of the Meuse-Argonne drive was to sweep the Germans back across the Meuse River from above Verdun to Mézières. A particularly vital target was the stretch of railroad that ran the twelve miles from Mézières to the rail division town of Sedan. To cut this line and force the Germans out of Sedan would not only drive a wedge between their left and right flanks but would hinder orderly withdrawal for a last-ditch stand on the Rhine.

Many of the Americans were green troops, but they were confident. Some of them had already tasted victory. In September, fighting for the first time as an American army—under General John J. Pershing—rather than as separate American divisions attached to French or British armies, they had conducted the offensive that wiped out the Germans' St.-Mihiel salient, to the southeast.

Facing them now was bad country, heavily fortified. The American left was in the Argonne Forest, a gloomy woodland seamed by ravines and hills, with bad roads—a worse place for an offensive, if possible, than even Virginia's famous Wilderness had been in the Civil War. East of the Argonne the country

MEUSE-ARGONNE OFFENSIVE
September 26 — November 11, 1918

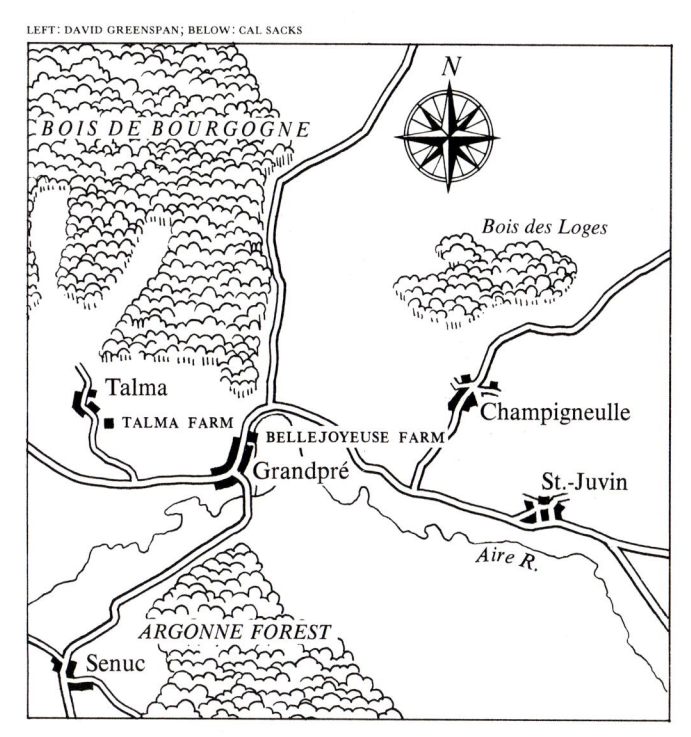

The whole Meuse-Argonne battlefield—as it might have been seen by a supercharged carrier pigeon flying at about 30,000 feet—is shown at left. The detail above represents the area outlined with the broken white line on the picture map. Here it was, in and around the town of Grandpré, between the Argonne Forest and the Bois de Bourgogne, that Sergeant Thomas J. Fleming's 78th Division fought the tumultuous actions described by his son in the accompanying article.

was more open, but no better. The German center was anchored on the imposing height of Montfaucon, with the valley of the Aire River going north some distance to the west. From Montfaucon to the Meuse there was more rough country, with the American right resting on the river a dozen miles north of historic Verdun. North of Montfaucon there were long hog-back ridges offering powerful defensive positions which the enemy had not overlooked.

In the first fifteen miles beyond the American front the Germans had built three chains of elaborate fortifications tied in with the famous Hindenburg Line. Together they presented an unending network of trenches, dugouts, barbed-wire entanglements, machine-gun nests, concrete bunkers, and fortified artillery batteries—as forbidding a prospect as any new army ever faced, or for that matter, any veteran army either.

The American offensive, which opened on September 26, threw nine American divisions into action. There is no space here to detail the separate engagements of the immense battle that followed, or to list the divisions that began it or the ones that were called to the front as the battle continued. What happened to Sergeant Fleming's 78th Division, as told in the accompanying AMERICAN HERITAGE story, was fairly typical of the whole tangled operation. In that difficult terrain, in that wet, cold, and foggy weather, and under the relentless harassment of German guns, it was inevitable that the offensive should be confused: some military historians have said that it was mismanaged. At any rate, it produced some of the legends of American military history—the "lost battalion," for instance, and the astonishing one-man show of Corporal Alvin York. (Corporal York, a sometime pacifist, more or less blundered into his capture of 132 German soldiers; but when he saw his opportunity, near the village of Cornay, he took it superbly.)

In the end, about all that can be said is that the advance kept going at terrible cost—117,000 American casualties in a little over six weeks. The frowning height of Montfaucon was taken; the wooded inferno of the Argonne was finally cleared out, yard by yard; eventually all the innumerable fortified positions that lay beyond were overrun. (On the map, the lines indicated by 1, 2, 3, and 4 show the positions of the American front on September 26, October 3, November 1, and November 11, respectively.) By November 11, the Americans and French had reached Sedan, and the war was over.

This of course is not to say that the Meuse-Argonne offensive was the blow that "won the war." The war was won by a number of blows, all of them essential to victory. This was one of them; a matter for somber pride to all Americans, because it showed that the fighting quality of the American soldier was as good as the best. —*Bruce Catton*

The morning after I arrived at Verdun I hired a car and guide and took the highway that runs north along the banks of the Meuse River, a curiously placid-looking stream only a few hundred yards wide, with low, almost nonexistent banks. The road passed French and German cemeteries, monuments to that earlier cataclysm, the year-long struggle for Verdun that consumed almost a million soldiers before America entered the war. When the road swung west across the Meuse I unfolded a multicolored map and asked eagerly: "Where's the Argonne?"

"The forest of the Argonne?" replied Robert Devillars, my guide. "That is many miles away. Let us first go to Montfaucon." Soon our little Renault was straining up an ever steeper hill; it finally groaned to a stop before a towering monument, a circular column of stone that rose 327 feet to a figure of Liberty at the summit. Immediately behind it were the ruins of a church and other buildings, the remains of the once-thriving village of Montfaucon.

From this steep-sided height I learned the first and most important lesson about the Argonne: its immensity. "See there," said M. Devillars. "There is the forest of the Argonne." My eyes strained toward a thin dark line on the western horizon. In between, the land rose and fell in a vast panorama of rolling hills and clumps of forest past the foot of Montfaucon to the banks of the Meuse.

The Argonne was not a battle for a forest. It was fought for the control of a region, of which the forest, stretching some fifteen miles along a dominating ridge, was the western boundary. From Montfaucon the vision of that September 26, 1918, dawn, when 225,000 Americans in nine divisions had surged forward, suddenly made a mockery of the word *personal*. From the New Yorkers of the 77th Division, thrashing through the Argonne Forest, to the Illinoisans of the 33rd Division, up to their cartridge belts in the oozing swamps along the Meuse, each unit experienced its own distinct version of hell. Did the single human being, the single regiment, even the single division, matter in such a cataclysm? I wondered, trying to see the whole stupendous scene with the historian's eye. Suddenly the answer was clear.

Yes.

Yes, because the very immensity of the experience staggered the mind. One could, of course, write an objective article about the Argonne, discussing the tactics, the progress made by the various divisions on the first, the second, the third, the fourth, the fifth, day. But to rescue the Argonne from this kind of abstract, impersonal history, to find its human dimension, it was absolutely necessary to reduce it to a smaller scale. Yes, I thought, returning to the car and driving down the hill toward the forest, coming here was not a mistake.

The intuition gathered momentum as we drove along the valley of the Aire River. It was a gray, sunless day, typical Argonne weather, and the landscape was in perfect harmony with the atonal sky. The Aire was as colorless as the back of a mirror and, seen from a distance, as inert as a dead snake. Dun-colored earth undulated to the right and left, broken by an occasional cluster of red-roofed farmhouses, or an isolated patch of woods. The long miles of open fields seemed peculiarly naked. The few fences were almost invisible wire, and there were no stone walls, no rocks, no hedges. It was all as bare as the Nebraska plain—but by no means as flat. Close up, the undulations became surprising hills or shallow ravines. It was a landscape in which only mass and density could make an impression, and the forest of the Argonne played this role with dark insistence. Mile after mile it was a brooding, impenetrable presence, on its twisting western height.

There in its little valley lay compact Varennes, famous in French history as the town where the fleeing Louis XVI was captured and sent back to Paris and his doom. Thousands of Pennsylvanians of the 28th Division died to drive the Germans out of it. A monument, one of the many that dot the Argonne region, commemorates their sacrifices. There was the village of Exermont, and that nearby narrow ravine where a German counterattack struck the exhausted, depleted Kansans and Missourians of the 35th Division on September 29, 1918, and almost turned the battle into a rout. There was Le Chene Tondue, a saw-toothed height jutting out of the Argonne Forest into the valley like the prow of a ship. From it German artillery dominated the lower half of both the valley and the forest. Next we passed the heights of Cornay and Châtel-Chéhéry, equally crucial to the upper half of the valley. Storming those nearly perpendicular slopes made men remember their elders' stories of Lookout Mountain and Cold Harbor in the Civil War. The divisions fighting east of the Aire had "scalloped" away these strong points at a terrible price, while across the valley other outfits swarmed up the steep slopes of Montfaucon. Both had to fight their way up a huge amphitheatre with enemies flinging destruction at them from three sides. Next we drove across the forest itself, pausing to stare down the shrouded slope where the famed "lost battalion" of the 77th Division was cut off but held out for five searing days against repeated German assaults. The round outlines of their foxholes are still visible after fifty years.

We were close to personal history now. The 78th Division had marched up through the Argonne's blasted, shell-stripped trees in the wake of the 77th. The Jerseyans had spent the two weeks preceding the Argonne buildup, and the first week of the battle itself, holding a sector of the St.-Mihiel line, about thirty miles to the southeast. To confuse the Germans about American intentions during the build-up, they had orders to keep the

CONTINUED ON PAGE 88

The Battle of the Fences

War appeals to something deep within the human soul, some philosophers say; otherwise we should not have so many of them. Whether or not this theory is valid, it is certainly true that, like dishwashers and detergents, wars must be advertised and sold. During World War I, before the spread of powerful mass media like the movies and radio, the poster on wall or fence was the most effective technique for mustering the people to total mobilization. Long before the United States entered the war, war posters had begun to appear in this country, as the democracies tried to enlist U.S. support and the imperial Central Powers tried to encourage our neutrality. Even the more specific posters, like Lloyd Myer's recruiting effort below, aimed at Englishmen abroad, carried what we now call subliminal appeal for the backing of America itself. And when we joined the Allies, the nation's artists rushed to their studios. The posters they produced, which we sample here, epitomize the needs and attitudes of a nation at war. They have echoes we can hear today. Co-ordinating the vast artistic effort of 1917 and 1918 was Charles Dana Gibson's Division of Pictorial Publicity, which valiantly waged the "Battle of the Fences" at weekly meetings in Keen's Chop House and later, as membership swelled, in the Salmagundi Club, both in New York City. There was a rebel, of course, and he was James Montgomery Flagg, who complained that Gibson "called meetings every time a cabin boy off a British ship appeared in our city. I soon became horribly bored with rising toasts." Flagg's authority for such disloyalty was, of course, his famous all-purpose poster above. Originally painted as a cover for *Leslie's Illustrated* (he posed for it himself), this poster saw action in both World Wars in more than four million copies. Gibson's group in nineteen months turned out 1,484 designs for posters, window cards, cartoons, seals, buttons, and banners —dramatic evidence, they insisted, that artists were not just long-haired Bohemians. Their victory dinner, held on February 14, 1919, at the Hotel Commodore, began, appropriately, with a Gibson cocktail. —R.S.G.

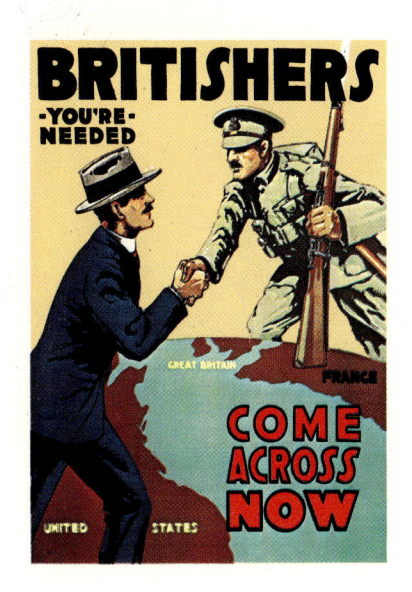

ALL POSTERS FROM THE COLLECTION OF THE NEW JERSEY HISTORICAL SOCIETY

For Home and Country

Family pride has traditionally served as an inducement to enlistment. What these two posters illustrate, however, is the contrast between the optimism of Alfred Everitt Orr's American recruiting ploy and the withering sarcasm expressed by an anonymous artist in England, where the casualty rate had depleted manpower reserves to the point where the "shirker" had become a national concern.

Daddy, what did _YOU_ do in the Great War?

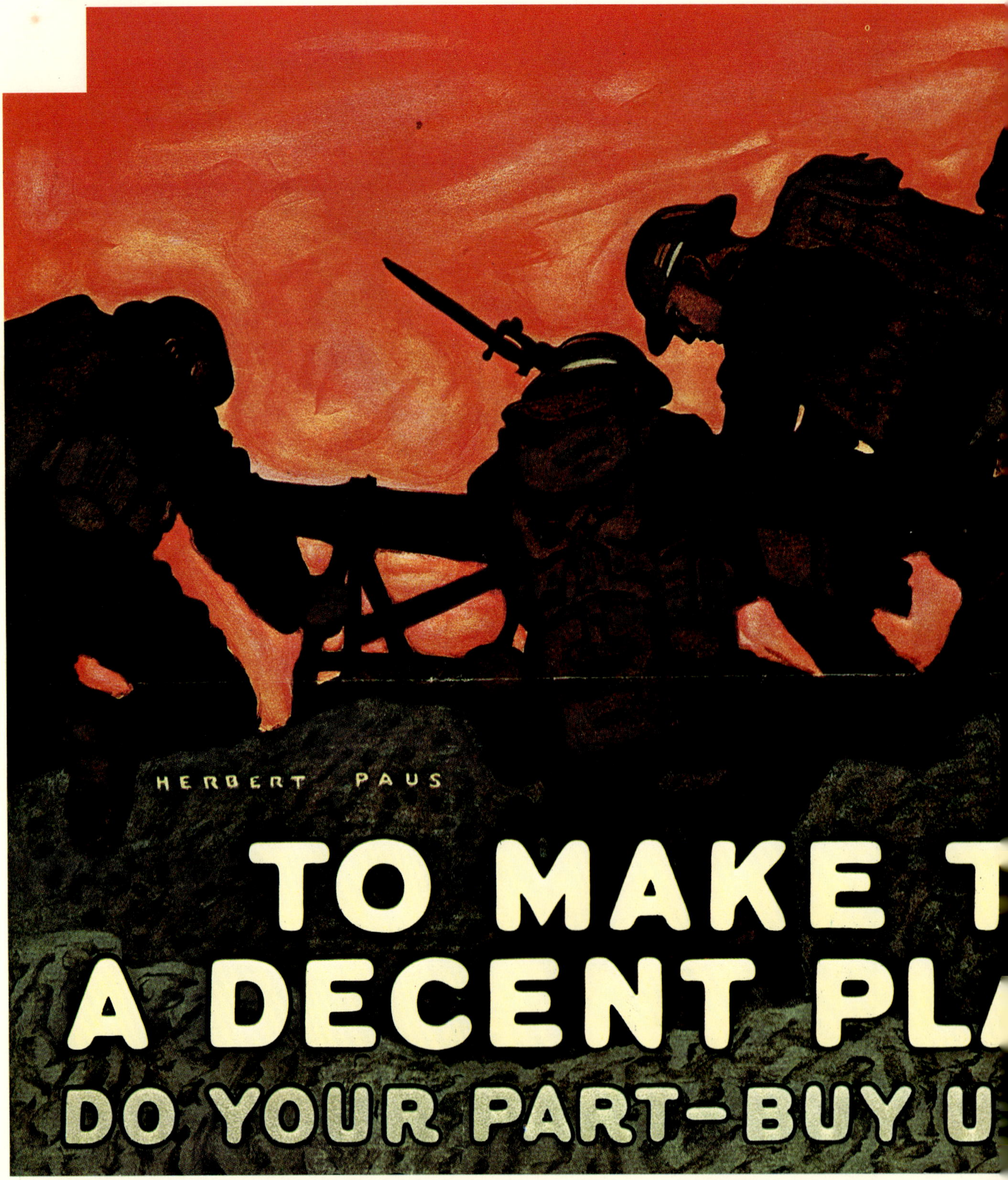
HERBERT PAUS
TO MAKE T
A DECENT PLA
DO YOUR PART-BUY U

The anomaly of combining Herbert Paus's silhouetted horrors of trench warfare with idealistic sentiments of intent is an example of how vastly different emotions can work effectively together. It also has the effect of emphasizing the awesome cost of securing the peace, which the viewer, far removed from the actual scene of the fighting, is invited to share through the purchase of war bonds.

Come On!
buy more LIBERTY BONDS

In poster warfare, naturally enough, your own side is brave to the point of heroism, as Walter Whitehead has shown above; the enemy comes off a blood-stained barbarian. The Hun at right is the work of F. Strothmann.

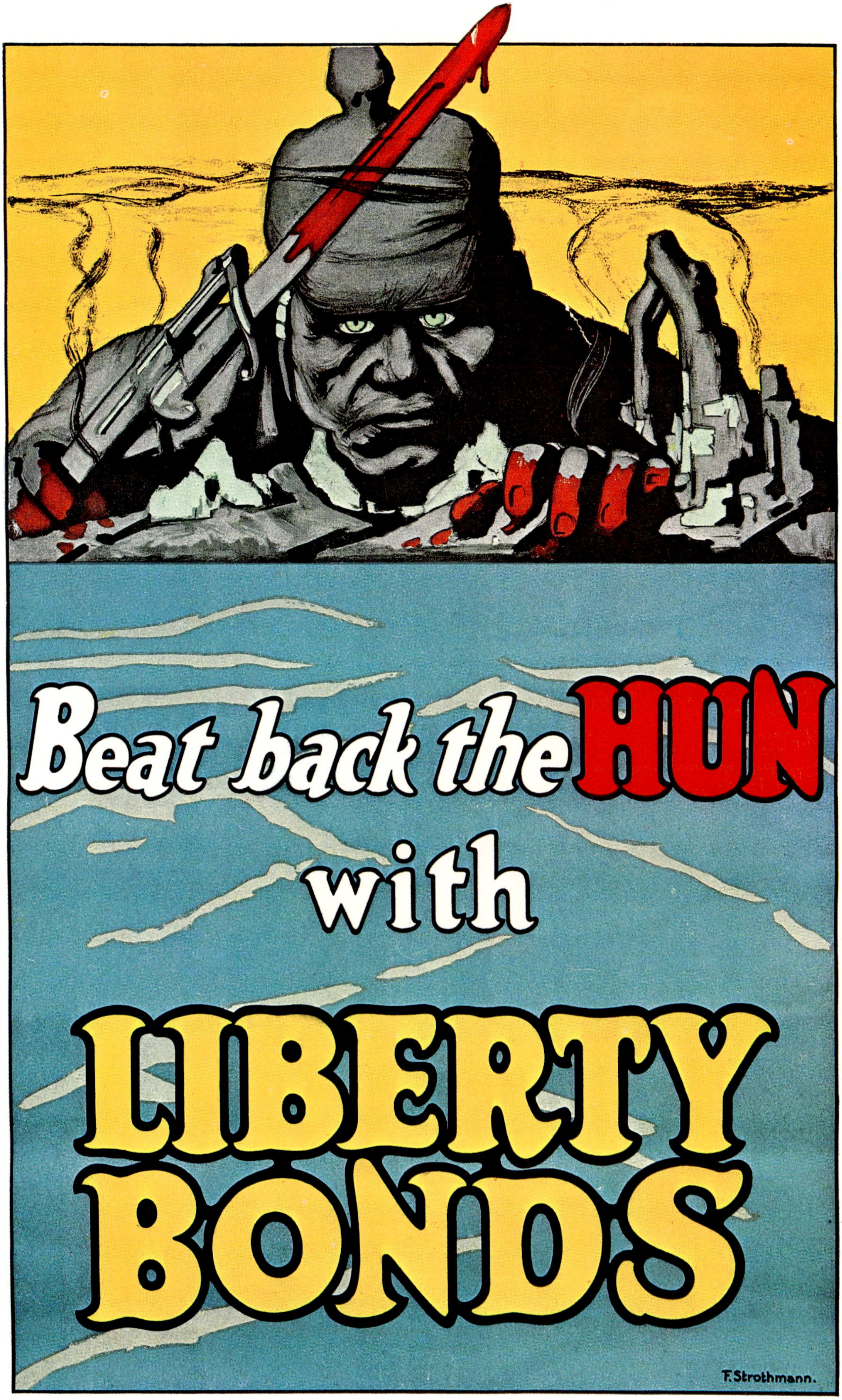
Beat back the HUN
with
LIBERTY
BONDS
F. Strothmann.

The appeal of sex in advertising gained impetus through war posters like these by Howard Chandler Christy and Harrison Fisher. In 1918, the very idea of dressing beautiful girls in chief petty officers' jackets or wrapping them in the American flag carried some rather sensational implications, the most obvious being that virility and patriotism were, at least for the duration of that great struggle, to be bedfellows.

"I Summon you to Comradeship in the Red Cross"
— Woodrow Wilson

Americans All!

Honor Roll

Du Bois
Smith
O'Brien
Cejka
Haucke
Pappandrikopolous
Andrassi
Villotto
Levy
Turovich
Kowalski
Chriczanevicz
Knutson
Gonzales

Howard Chandler Christy, 1919

Everyone, we trust, remembers the typical bomber crew of World War II, as brought to us by Hollywood—the Boston Irishman, the wise-guy WASP from Texas, the unpronounceable Polack from South Bend, the philosophical Jewish chap from Brooklyn, the ... but why go on? Here they all are, a whole war earlier, in Howard Chandler Christy's poster at left. And his Liberty was everyone's ideal of a smashing girl, as opposed to the marble-faced ladies of silver coins and the harbor. Below, the melting-pot syndrome reappears in a poster by Charles E. Chambers.

FOOD WILL WIN THE WAR
You came here seeking Freedom
You must now help to preserve it

STOP

SAVE
Prune pits
Plum pits
Cherry pits
Date seeds
Olive pits
Peach Stones
Apricot pits
the shells of
Hickory nuts
Butternuts and
Walnuts

The carbon produced from these materials when placed in respirators will

SAVE SOLDIERS' LIVES
by absorbing
GERMAN POISON GAS

DRY MATERIALS THOROUGHLY AND DELIVER TO POINTS DESIGNATED BY
THE AMERICAN RED CROSS
DO YOUR BIT — SAVE THE PIT

GAS DEFENSE DIVISION · CHEMICAL WARFARE SERVICE U.S.A.

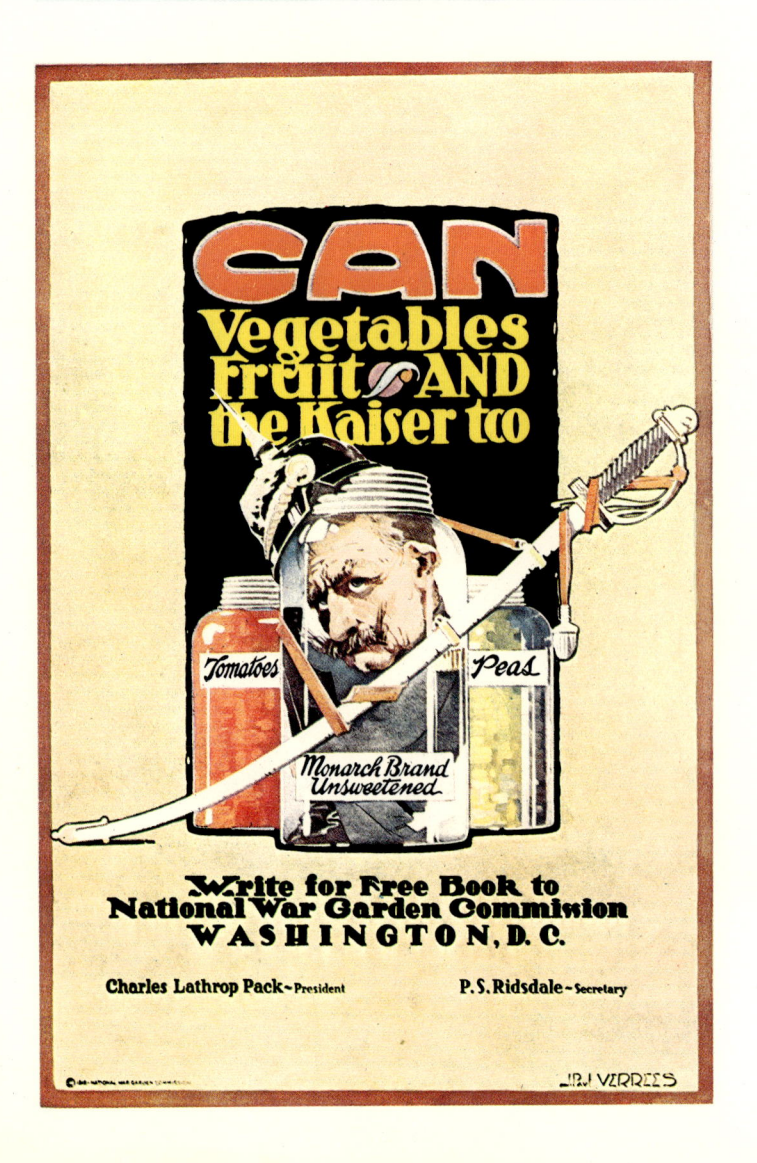

KNIT A BIT
FOR OUR FIRST LINE OF DEFENSE
WOOL, NEEDLES AND DIRECTIONS
Comforts Committee of the Navy League
OF THE UNITED STATES
509 FIFTH AVENUE, NEW YORK CITY

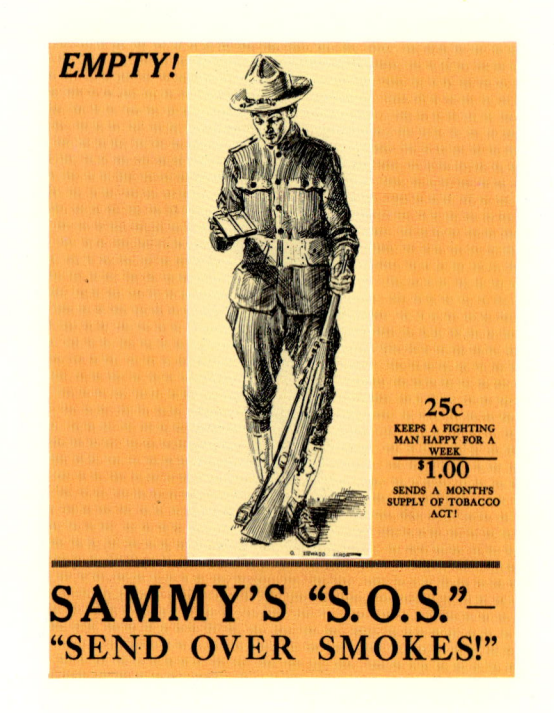

CAN
Vegetables
Fruit AND
the Kaiser too

Tomatoes   Peas
Monarch Brand
Unsweetened

Write for Free Book to
National War Garden Commission
WASHINGTON, D.C.

Charles Lathrop Pack ~ President   P. S. Ridsdale ~ Secretary

---

EMPTY!

25c
KEEPS A FIGHTING
MAN HAPPY FOR A
WEEK

$1.00
SENDS A MONTH'S
SUPPLY OF TOBACCO
ACT!

SAMMY'S "S.O.S."—
"SEND OVER SMOKES!"

This selection of home-front posters suggests only a few of the unending variety of ways to win a war—one of the most crucial of which is to keep the civilian population constantly conscious that a war is going on. At times it must have seemed as if there were more causes than people. One obvious change over the intervening years is that it is no longer possible to keep a fighting man in cigarettes—even with the new extra-long, super-king-size varieties—for an entire month on just one dollar.
Overleaf: Rosie the Riveter of World War II was still in diapers when Jonas Lie painted this bustling shipyard, as America rushed, then as it would again, to build a mighty merchant marine.

This Girl Is Doing War Work for Uncle Sam

Will You Rent Her A Room?

SAVING DAYLIGHT!

UNCLE SAM, YOUR ENEMIES HAVE BEEN UP AND ARE AT WORK ON THE EXTRA HOUR OF DAYLIGHT— WHEN WILL YOU WAKE UP?

United Cigar Stores Company

We Eat because we Work

We belong to the U.S. School Garden Army

ISSUED BY THE U.S. SCHOOL GARDEN ARMY BUREAU OF EDUCATION, DEPARTMENT OF INTERIOR. WASHINGTON, D.C.

"HELP THE HORSE TO SAVE THE SOLDIER"

"GOOD-BYE, OLD MAN"

PLEASE JOIN THE AMERICAN RED STAR ANIMAL RELIEF National Headquarters, Albany, N.Y.

ON THE JOB

OR VICTORY

THAT LIBERTY SHALL NOT PERISH FROM THE EARTH BUY LIBERTY BONDS

This apocalyptic view of New York City by Joseph Pennell seems to belong to a future we hope never comes, but it dates to World War I.

AMERICAN HERITAGE
BOOK SELECTION

A FAR-FLUNG PEOPLE

The Eskimo were the first inhabitants of the New World to be seen by Europeans, for the Vikings encountered them at least as early as 1005, probably on the southeast coast of Labrador. Surprisingly, the numerous Norse sagas made little mention of them at first. But within another two centuries the Eskimo were already being described with the exaggeration and lack of understanding that later came to typify the European's view of the natives of the New World. The anonymous author of the thirteenth-century *Historia Norvegiae* wrote: "Hunters have found some very little people, whom they call Skraelings, and who, when they are wounded with weapons while still alive, die without loss of blood, but whose blood, when they are dead, will not cease to flow."

Nor does much reliable information exist about the numbers of Eskimo. The population probably was never very high, perhaps 100,000 or so at its maximum, but soon after contact with whites the number of Eskimo plummeted because of epidemics of measles, smallpox, and other European diseases that they had not previously encountered and to which they therefore had no immunity. The Eskimo population is believed to have risen again in this century to an estimated 73,000, living from extreme northeastern Siberia across Alaska and Canada to Greenland.

The Eskimo today inhabit the broadest stretch of land of any primitive people on earth. They circle nearly half the globe along the Arctic coast, a distance of some six thousand twisting and turning miles. This is a considerably smaller area than they inhabited in aboriginal times, however, for in the seventeenth century the Eskimo were reported as far south as the Gulf of St. Lawrence, and there is archeological evidence of their having once inhabited a large part of eastern Siberia (about fifteen hundred or so Eskimo still live in Soviet Russia). No other primitive people spread out over such a wide area has ever shown an equal uniformity in physical type, language, and culture. They everywhere refer to themselves as *inuit*, which is simply the plural of *inuk*, "man," and in that way they emphasize their own identity in contrast to the Indians around them, who differ in physical type, lan-

The unique, durable culture of the Eskimo included settling arguments with song and sharing wives among friends

By PETER FARB

COPYRIGHT © 1968 BY PETER FARB

guage, and culture. The white man's name, Eskimo, was coined in 1611 by a Jesuit who heard them called *eskimantsik,* which means "eaters of raw meat," by neighboring Indians. No matter where they live, most Eskimo are readily identifiable by their stocky build, long heads and short faces, and narrow slanting eyelids with the Mongoloid fold. Their dialects, with the exception of a few in Siberia and in Alaska, are mutually intelligible; a new song or joke introduced into Alaska makes its way from one scattered camp to another and may turn up in Greenland a year or so later. Those few Eskimo who have not yet entered the white man's economy still base their subsistence, in the traditional way, on hunting.

A common thread running through all Eskimo cultures was adaptation to the stern arctic environment. The latitudes inhabited by the Eskimo are marked by enormous differences between summer and winter. During the winter the sun does not shine for weeks; during the summer it never sets. Summer is the only time when the mean daily temperatures rise above freezing, but it is also the season of biting flies and of melted water lying over the tundra without draining away, forming an impenetrable morass. Tree growth is impossible under such conditions, and only in a few places occupied by the Eskimo do even low tangles of willow and alder grow. For his supply of wood, the Eskimo had to rely on the drift brought into the Arctic Ocean by rivers that drain the interiors of Northern America and Asia.

Despite these unpromising conditions, the material culture of the Eskimo has always shown a more complex development than that of any other primitive people living on such a simple level as the family. They take advantage of almost one hundred per cent of the potential of their forbidding environment. Everyone has heard of at least some of their adaptations. The igloo, or snow house, was the best possible structure that could be built with the materials available; it was strong, easily constructed, and durable. Some Eskimo used the dog sled and the kayak, and they tailored their clothes so that the seams were waterproof. Slit goggles were made from ivory to protect against the blinding sun reflected from the snow. Deprived of wood for heating and light, they invented the smokeless stone lamp that burned seal oil. They even devised a beater for removing snow, and thus prevented fur clothing from deteriorating in the humid atmosphere of the igloo.

Anyone who has seen the tools and weapons of the Eskimo in a museum knows how carefully they are made. Often these objects are also beautiful, a fact that has interesting implications for theories about the beginnings of art. In the far North, where man had to face the constant threat of starvation, where life was reduced to the bare essentials, it turns out that one of these essentials was art. Samuel Hearne, an eighteenth-century Hudson's Bay Company trader, in midwinter in the desolate Canadian tundra came upon the tracks of a snowshoe with an unfamiliar shape. He followed the trail to a little hut; inside he found a lone woman who explained that she had been kidnapped by another band but had escaped seven months previously. Since that time she had lived alone, supporting herself by snaring what small game she could. Hearne wrote:

> It is scarcely possible to conceive that a person in her forlorn situation could be so composed as to contrive or execute anything not absolutely essential to her existence. Nevertheless, all her clothing, besides being calculated for real service, showed great taste, and no little variety of ornament. The materials, though rude, were very curiously wrought, and so judiciously placed as to make the whole of her garb have a very pleasing, though rather romantic appearance.

An inventory of Eskimo technology could be extended for pages, but such a catalogue would not convey the meaning of Eskimo inventiveness. One can measure, describe, photograph, and make a diagram of a kayak, for instance, and he can even transport it to a museum. But no matter how perfect his kayak specimen is, he still has not captured the reality of kayak-ness. To grasp this reality one must understand that every bit as important as the wooden frames and skin cover of the canoe are other essentials: who owned it, who was allowed to ride in it, what taboos were connected with it, what rituals governed its launching

While one Eskimo cut the slabs of hard-packed snow of which the igloo was constructed, another fitted them into place.

and its use, and so on. The same principle applies to all other aspects of Eskimo material culture.

The Eskimo were once considered a classic example of a people molded by their physical environment. Although now rejected as fallacious by almost all anthropologists, this old theory of "environmental determinism" nevertheless has subtly entered our way of thinking. One still hears some educated people maintain that Massachusetts has produced more scholars than Alabama because the long, snowbound winters afford New Englanders greater opportunity for uninterrupted study. It *is* true that Massachusetts has produced many more scholars than Alabama, but not because of the climate or any other aspect of the physical environment. Other factors—the superior educational system in Massachusetts, the earlier founding of its schools, the intellectual receptivity of its settlers, and so forth—are much more important than the long winters. If any connection did exist between long winters and scholarship, then the Eskimo surely should have produced even more scholars than the people of Massachusetts.

Of course, natural surroundings do influence the broad outlines of a culture: an Eskimo inhabitant of the Arctic could no more become an agriculturist than a Pueblo Indian of the Arizona or New Mexican desert could base his economy on harpooning walruses. But the environment did not determine the Eskimo's culture; it merely set the outer limits and at the same time offered opportunities. Such limits and opportunities of physical environment are felt in varying ways by different peoples, depending upon their level of culture. Drought represented a disaster to a Shoshone band of the Great Basin in Utah or Nevada. But inhabiting an equally arid environment in Mexico were the Mixtec, a culturally advanced people who had largely liberated themselves from their environment by the construction of irrigation works. To the Mixtec, drought was simply a hardship which they soon overcame.

The Arctic demonstrates with almost textbook clarity the fallacy of environmental determinism—for if man has been able to make different kinds of adjustments there, then it is clear that environment influences cultures only in the most general way. The North American Eskimo exploited the arctic environment with ingenuity, as his igloo, sled, harpoon, and snow goggles attest. In the Siberian Arctic, just across the Bering Strait, the environment is exactly the same and the land was inhabited by close relatives of the Eskimo known as the Chukchi—yet the Chukchi evolved quite a different kind of culture. The Chukchi did not make igloos; instead, they built dwellings by attaching skins to wooden frameworks, even though wood was as scarce in the land of the Chukchi as it was in the land of the Eskimo. Nor were the Chukchi very proficient hunters. Before the coming of whites, the Eskimo hunted caribou (reindeer), whereas the Chukchi herded them. In fact, the Chukchi adapted to the arctic environment just as successfully as the Eskimo—but they did so in almost opposite ways.

Interest in the harsh envrionment of the Eskimo and the drama of his response to it has blinded us to other important things that the Eskimo can reveal about man. The material technology of the Eskimo, sophisticated as it was within its narrow limits, may obscure the primitive reality of the Eskimo's life. Less dramatic, but ultimately more important, were the Eskimo's *social* adaptations, his customs and laws and religion.

The Eskimo's precarious existence placed certain demands upon him. The primary one was to find a way to survive in small and isolated groups and at the same time preserve his mobility. Because the Eskimo fed mostly on migratory animals rather than stationary plants, every morsel that entered his mouth had to be sought out, often over great distances. (He was able to dispense with plant food because he ate at least half of his meat raw, and that half included the fat and the internal organs of the animal. With such a diet, he obtained from the meat every vitamin and mineral, as well as all the protein, necessary for human nutrition.) The Eskimo improved upon the lot of most primitive hunters by devising sleds, but even so, the amount that he could transport was small.

Because of the extremely low population density,

Having adapted differently than the Eskimo, the Chukchi of the Siberian Arctic domesticated reindeer and lived in tents.

67

contacts between families were rare; the local group that came together during the winter was usually composed of fewer than a dozen families, perhaps related, although actual kinship was not emphasized. The only leadership in these groups of families was that of a mentor, or headman (whose title in the Eskimo language means "he who knows best"). He obtained his position solely by achievement: he did not campaign for it, nor could he pass on the office to his sons or other relatives. In a republic of equals, he was only slightly more equal than others. The family group usually did not have definite marriage or residence rules. Among Eskimo groups, the older sons might have lived with the father and the younger sons might have lived with their wives' families. Religious ceremonies were rarely concerned with the group as a whole, but rather with the rites of passage of the individual: birth, puberty, and death.

Yet certain factors tended to unite families. Among the Copper Eskimo of Canada, for example, the inhabitants of a settlement were all connected by blood or by marriage. Each owed special duties to the others: to care for them in sickness, to feed the aged and the infirm, to protect widows and orphans. In this way, a group of separate families took on a loose corporate unity. It eventually was referred to by a common name, which was usually the suffix *miut* added to the name of a prominent topographical feature in the region it inhabited. *Kogluktokmiut*, therefore, was the name of the group that frequented the Kogluktok, or Coppermine, River. Physical propinquity, a similarity in habits and dialect, and intermarriage gave them a sense of closeness that set them off from neighboring Eskimo groups.

Marriage was at the center of Eskimo life, even though some explorers have concluded that because of wife swapping and other sexual irregularities the Eskimo did not much revere the institution. But the Eskimo was enthusiastically in favor of marriage. A man married just as soon as he could hunt with sufficient skill to feed a wife, and girls often married before they reached puberty. A man was destitute without a wife. He had no one to make his clothes or to cook for him. A woman without a husband lived like a beggar, for she had no one to hunt game for her. Marriage was simply an economic necessity, and so there were no elaborate courtship displays or marriage celebrations among the Eskimo. A man and a woman arranged to live together, the agreement occasioning less pomp than a modern American displays when he hires a carpenter.

The thing that most bewildered the prudish white about the Eskimo's connubial eccentricities—wife lending, wife swapping, polyandry, and polygyny—was the good nature with which the arrangements were made. Occasionally an Eskimo man would beat his wife for being unfaithful—not because she had had sexual intercourse with someone else, but because she had taken it upon herself to grant rights that were the husband's privilege to bestow. The next week he himself might have lent her to the same man. Wife exchange existed to some extent in all Eskimo groups that have been studied; the explanation is that such an exchange was one of the best ways to formalize an economic partnership or a social alliance. With so few opportunities existing to create bonds between families, the Eskimo had to use ingenuity, and one of the best methods was exchanging sexual rights.

Wife lending and wife exchange must therefore be understood not as examples of sexual license but as clever social mechanisms that functioned to unify small groups. Further, wife lending was a wise investment for the future, because the lender knew that eventually he would be a borrower. Perhaps he had to go on a long journey and his wife could not accompany him because she was sick or pregnant; then he borrowed his friend's wife. He was not a lecher who wanted a woman, but a man who needed such essential services as cooking and serving. While he was out hunting, his friend's wife made the igloo habitable, laid out dry stockings for him, made fresh water from melted ice, and got ready to cook the game he brought back. Similarly, polyandry and polygyny were essential, for a lone Eskimo could not survive. He or she had to become attached to some family.

Wife exchange usually was an essential ritual in the formation of an economic partnership between hunters. When two men agreed to become partners, they

The Eskimo made their sleds, indispensable to their nomadic lives, of whalebone or wood lashed together with hide. The runners were rimmed with extra hard bone and made slippery by a coating of fresh-water ice. A pair of deer antlers was often attached to the sled to form a back rest.

symbolically extended the bonds of kinship to each other. They became in effect related by marriage by the act of exchanging wives for a while. In northern Alaska in particular, wives were exchanged as a sort of attestation to the formation of a partnership. The wives rarely objected, since, among other reasons, each stood to profit economically because of her husband's new economic bond. The partnership arrangement also extended to the children. A child called his father's partner by a special name, which freely translated means "the man who has had intercourse with my mother." The child also used a special name—*qatangun*—for his father's partner's sons, who might, of course, be his half brothers. He knew that if he was ever in trouble he could call on his qatangun for help and his request would be honored.

Exchange was a necessity of Eskimo life that applied to things as well as wives. The explorers of North America made much of what seemed to them an inordinate preoccupation by the Eskimo with gift giving. Over and over the explorers related their disillusionment when the Eskimo failed to have the "courtesy" to thank them for gifts. And the explorers also invariably expressed amazement that their unacknowledged gifts were later remembered and repaid in full. The explorers merely regarded gift giving as a quaint Eskimo custom and did not recognize it as a type of exchange.

When one Eskimo gave to another in his band, he was usually giving to a relative or to a partner. Such an exchange was not a gift, and that was why the receiver did not offer thanks. An Eskimo praised a hunter for the way he hurled the harpoon but not for the way he shared the meat from the seal the harpoon killed. Sharing was a kinsman's due, and it was not in the category of a gift. The arctic explorer Peter Freuchen once made the mistake of thanking an Eskimo hunter, with whom he had been living, for some meat. Freuchen's bad manners were promptly corrected: "You must not thank for your meat; it is your right to get parts. In this country, nobody wishes to be dependent upon others. . . . With gifts you make slaves just as with whips you make dogs!"

An important point about exchange in the life of the Eskimo was that he alternated between feast and famine. One Eskimo hunter might be successful in killing seal after seal while another hunter was having a long streak of bad luck. Anyone who has been molded by a capitalistic culture knows what he might do in similar circumstances; if he were the fortunate hunter and the others were in need, he might jack up prices. Such a thing never happened in Eskimo society—not because an Eskimo was innately nobler than you or I, but because an Eskimo knew that despite his plenty today, assuredly he would be in want tomorrow. He knew also that the best place for him to store his surplus was in someone else's stomach, because sooner or later he would want his gift repaid. Pure selfishness gave the Eskimo a reputation for generosity and earned him the good opinion of missionaries and other observers who hunger after proof of the innate goodness of man.

The Eskimo male from time to time engaged in conflicts, often violent ones, and surprisingly enough, the usual cause was adultery. It was not considered adultery when a husband lent his wife to a friend. Nor was it considered adultery when a husband and wife joined other couples in the game known as "putting out the lamp"—during which period of darkness they picked at random a partner of the opposite sex. Adultery existed only when a woman had sexual intercourse without the express approval and prior knowledge of her husband. Since such approval could usually be had for the asking, adultery had a significance other than sexual gratification. It was one man's unspoken challenge to another. And the offended husband had to respond to that challenge or else he would live out the rest of his years in shame.

Murder was almost always the outcome of such a challenge to status. When the arctic explorer Knud Rasmussen visited a community of fifteen Eskimo families in the early 1920's, he found that every one of the adult males had committed homicide at least once, and in every case the apparent motive had been a quarrel about a woman. It would, however, be a mistake to think that an Eskimo was more preoccupied with usurpation of sexual rights than other people are. The Eskimo's problem lay in his society, which possessed no clear-cut laws governing marriage and divorce. Marriage was simply living together; divorce was simply ceasing to live together. In arrangements as informal as these, no way existed to determine when someone was trespassing on another's rights. Since in Eskimo society things were always being borrowed, there was no definition of where borrowing of a wife ended and appropriation of her began. When a wife was borrowed, she did not leave the premises with a return date like a library book. Judgment and good taste alone determined how soon she would be returned.

The murder, either of the interloper or of the injured husband, had to be revenged by the kinsmen of the murdered man, and this in turn often resulted in further retaliation. There was no chivalry or bravery involved in blood revenge: in all Eskimo communities except those of western Greenland, it was carried out by stealth. Since a murderer was required to care for the widow and the children of his victim, blood revenge sometimes created a ludicrous situation. A murderer reared as his own stepson the son of his victim—and when this boy grew to manhood he might be the very one to exact delayed blood vengeance upon his foster father.

Several mechanisms served as checks on the proliferation of killings and revenge. The Eskimo realized that feuds were potentially dangerous to their existence, and families were quick to punish the wrongdoers in their own ranks. Every attempt was made to prevent a quarrel from leading to murder. As soon as a quarrel became public knowledge, other people in the group sought out a kinsman common to both parties to adjudicate. A man who had murdered several times became an object of concern to the entire group. An executioner obtained in advance the community's approval—including that of the family of the inveterate murderer—for doing away with this social menace. No revenge could be taken on the executioner, for he was acting in the name of all the people.

There were other outlets for ending quarrels short of actual murder: buffeting, butting, wrestling, and song duels. In buffeting, the opponents faced each other and in turn gave forceful blows until one was felled. In butting, the opponents struck at each other with their foreheads, and the one who was knocked down was derided by the onlookers. Wrestling might seem safe enough, but it occasionally had a deadly outcome, and it was one of the subtler ways of carrying out blood revenge. Such contests were announced in advance, and they took place before the whole group, which regarded them as festive occasions. Regardless of the underlying justice of the case in dispute, the winner was the one who possessed the greater strength. Justice was irrelevant to the outcome, and the victor won not only the case but also social esteem.

In Alaska and in Greenland all except lethal disputes were settled by a song duel. In these areas an Eskimo male was often as acclaimed for his ability to sing insults as for his hunting prowess. The song duel consisted of lampoons, insults, and obscenities that the disputants sang to each other and, of course, to their delighted audience. The verses were earthy and very much to the point; they were intended to humiliate, and no physical deformity, personal shame, or family trouble was exempt. As verse after verse was sung in turn by the opponents, the audience began to take sides; it applauded one singer a bit longer and laughed a bit louder at his lampoons. Finally, he was the only one to get applause, and he thereby became the winner of a bloodless contest. The loser suffered a great punishment, for disapproval of the community was very difficult to bear in a group as small as that of the Eskimo. Prestige is a precious thing to an Eskimo, as the following incident emphasizes. Among the Chugach Eskimo, a thief once entered a house in which an old woman was eating. She began to sing:

Old Turd, Old Turd.
He makes me ashamed.
He was looking at me when I was eating.
Old Turd, Old Turd.

This song may not appear particularly clever, but it was sufficient to make the thief leave the house without taking anything. Soon the children in the band sang the song whenever they saw him. The result was that he was cured of stealing.

The absence among the Eskimo and other primitive peoples of our conventional concepts of property has been the source of some theories that communism is a basic condition of mankind. But do the facts really warrant such a conclusion? The Eskimo had two kinds of property: communal and personal—but they lacked private property. The natural resources on which the band depended—the rivers filled with fish, the tundra where the caribou fed, the shores of the sea in which seals lived—were communal and open to use by all members of the band. Personal property consisted of things made by individuals: weapons, tools, ornaments, fetishes, and so forth. These items were not really private property, because they belonged not to the individual himself but to his *role* in Eskimo society. It was preposterous that an Eskimo woman, who had a specific role, should own a harpoon, even though she may have been foolish enough to devote her energies to making one. Nor was the concept of personal

Whenever they could, Eskimo hunters chased reindeer into the water, where in their swift kayaks they could more easily overtake and spear the slowly swimming animals.

ownership very far-reaching: it was unthinkable that one Eskimo should possess two harpoons while a less fortunate kinsman lacked even one.

Since no private property existed among the Eskimo, it would appear that they were communistic. But to believe so would be to miss an important point about primitive society. Communism, as the word is understood in modern society, refers to ownership by *all* the citizens of the means of production and an absence of exploitive relations. In modern communism, the "all" refers to the entire population, related or not. But who were the "all" in Eskimo society? Almost everyone was related by blood or by marriage or as an economic partner. The Eskimo group was really one big family that included also close friends (in the same way that an American child might call his parents' friend "aunt," even though she is not a relative). Even in the capitalistic United States, most families practice this same sort of "communism" of the family: they are generous to children, indulgent to nephews and nieces, hospitable to cousins.

Someone reared in the context of Western civilization will also find the spiritual beliefs of the Eskimo considerably different from the religions he is used to. Eskimo belief was among the simplest known, and it incorporated the two common denominators of all religions everywhere—spirits and magic. It completely lacked all the other ideas of religion found in advanced societies: revelation, a redeemer, a priesthood, orthodox rituals, articles of faith, and so on. Probably the Eskimo spiritual beliefs did not differ much from man's earliest gropings toward religion, but that will never be known for sure.

The debate as to where "magic" ends and "religion" begins is an old one that seemed settled some decades ago when scholars concluded that there was no discernible boundary between them. As a result, the two were often lumped together as "magico-religious," in much the same way that the compromise word "sociocultural" originated. Nevertheless, at least one distinction must be made between magic and religion. In magic, the practitioner believes that he can directly affect other humans and nature, either for good or for ill, by performing certain steps. Magic is therefore instrumental—and some of these instruments are witchcraft, sorcery, oracles, divination, and various kinds of curing. Although many "religious" people do use religion for instrumental ends, the primary emphasis in religion is on broad social and cosmological relationships.

Eskimo magic differed from Christianity, Judaism, Mohammedanism, and Buddhism in that it did not attempt to regulate behavior in the society as a whole or to propagate a code of conduct and belief. It was not interested in the totality of the invisible world, but was instead limited to the individual's relationship to his food supply and to his physical environment. The Eskimo's magic operated through an elaborate system of hundreds of taboos that constrained his every action. Knud Rasmussen once asked a wise Igulik Eskimo, "What do you believe?" "We don't believe," he answered. "We only fear." This sums up the attitude of the Eskimo as well as of other peoples in simple societies. They lived in a world of anxiety, frustration, inadequacy, and vulnerability, in which the spirits controlled everything that could not be explained rationally. The modern American, of course, does not suffer the same kind of anxiety, since he has exerted technological control over many of the things that make the Eskimo fearful. In place of science, the Eskimo had only magic to bridge the gap between what he could and could not understand. Without magic, his life would have been one long panic.

The taboos had to be scrupulously observed. To violate one was a sin. However, the Eskimo feeling about sin was notable in that it lacked any holier-than-thou attitude. The group did not revel in an upwelling of indignation; there were no righteous lectures, no public stonings of miscreants. Instead, the community united in compassion and tolerance around the sinner. He was encouraged to purge his sin, and he did so by hiring a part-time religious practitioner known as a shaman, who drew forth from the sinner's mouth the details of each taboo violation. The villagers sat in the background, chanting cries of forgiveness.

To harpoon a seal, the Eskimo hunter would lie motionless on the ice for hours, looking seallike himself. When the seal slept or looked away, the hunter crept up for the kill.

Illness in the soul of the wrongdoer was usually the result of sin—but the Eskimo also believed that illness might result from the witchcraft of a malevolent shaman. Witchcraft was not head-to-head butting or even murder by stealth, but evil worked in the privacy of one's own igloo. Social scientists used to think that witchcraft was correlated with the food supply: the more precarious a group's food supply, the more prevalent the fear of sorcery. But this is not true. Compared with the Eskimo, the Navaho of Arizona and New Mexico lived in luxury, yet they were even more haunted by witchcraft. When an Eskimo fell sick and attributed his sickness to witchcraft by a hostile shaman, he felt that he had probably done something to the shaman that could not be settled publicly by a song duel or even by murder. In such a case, the ill person had to fight poison with poison, so he hired a friendly shaman to locate the secret attacker and nullify his power.

Eskimo belief provides an explanation of what witchcraft is really all about: it is aggression for which a society has not provided channels. In fact, an examination of witchcraft in primitive societies around the world shows that it appears when people attempt to handle their vital problems in the absence of legitimate social controls. What is surprising about witchcraft in Eskimo society is not that it existed, but that it was not much more prevalent. This was due to the various social constraints mentioned earlier: public ridicule, prestige, the use of kinsmen in settling quarrels, a public executioner, and so forth. Although these are not our familiar social controls of law, courts, and the police, they served somewhat the same function.

The only division of labor in many Eskimo bands was by age or by sex—except for the role of shaman. The word *shaman* comes from the Tungus language of Siberia, but the shaman was important among all the Eskimo bands and among many American Indian groups, particularly in the West (where he was usually called a "medicine man" by whites). Wherever he existed, the shaman moved with ease in the supernatural realm. He was in the business of going to the invisible world and contending with the spirits on their own ground. An Eskimo believed that spirits must be coerced; a widespread myth told how the sea spirit Sedna had to be harpooned to force her to release sea mammals for the hunt.

There is a vast difference between a shaman and a priest. A priest is a legally constituted specialist; he belongs to a special group set apart from the rest of the social organization. An Eskimo shaman, on the other hand, dressed no differently from anyone else, and he lived like the rest of the community. He hunted, or he joined a whaling crew; he could marry and sire children. He had no special privileges or insignia, except the tambourine, a skin drum open on one side, that all Eskimo shamans used while singing.

There were, however, ways to recognize him. Search out the least skilled hunter in the group, one who was also physically or mentally handicapped and who made nervous movements with his hands or feet. This was undoubtedly the man. The shaman actually was different from everybody else, and the Eskimo was smart enough to recognize this and put it to work in his society. Some Eskimo maintained that they could identify a future shaman, even while he was still a child, by certain signs. He was meditative and introverted; he might have been subject to fits or fainting spells; he was disturbed by dreams and he suffered from hallucinations and hysteria. The shaman was a psychological type known as the neurotic, borderline schizoid —which was perfectly all right with the Eskimo, who believed the shaman needed extraordinary abilities in his traffic with the supernatural. The shaman came to the fore because Eskimo culture encouraged his hallucinations, created such situations as the curing ceremonies in which he could flourish, and even rewarded him when his symptoms appeared.

Some anthropologists have stated that the shaman filled an important function by draining off the potential "arctic hysteria" of the group. But it was not so simple as that, and the shaman may have actually represented the element of hostility in Eskimo culture. The person who became a shaman was almost always more misanthropic, more covertly aggressive, and less physically skilled than the ordinary man. The things the shaman himself hated—the successful hunter, the

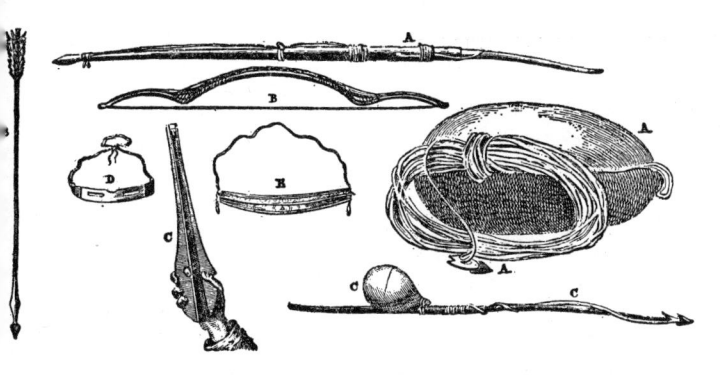

*The woman at left is softening a boot by chewing it, the traditional Eskimo method of making leather pliable. The ancient Eskimo tools shown in the eighteenth-century engraving above are: **A**–at top, a whale harpoon and, at right, its barbed tip and the line and buoy the Eskimo attached to it; **B**–a bow and arrow; **C**–a seal harpoon with a bladder to impede the seal's swimming and, at left, a hand-held device for firing it. **D** is snow goggles; **E**, a breast ornament.*

virile man with many women, the boatowner with his prestige—were things the rest of the group envied also. Unlike the ordinary Eskimo, the shaman could do something about his malevolence: he could call down sickness upon the envied one. If a skilled hunter suddenly was unable to find game, he might attribute his misfortune not to chance but to the malefic influence of some shaman or other. He then employed his local shaman to perform an emotional ceremony that removed the evil influence. The hunter emerged from the experience a more humble man; he was careful to stop boasting of his hunting skill, to leave game for others, to share more. The shaman and the rest of the Eskimo group had the satisfaction of seeing the mighty brought low.

Were the shamans frauds? Shamans used many tricks to heighten the effects of their performances: ventriloquism, hypnosis, legerdemain, and general stage magic. Houdini-like escapes were a specialty. A shaman often impressed his audience by vomiting blood; he did this by previously swallowing a bladder filled with animal blood, then breaking it with his stomach muscles at the appropriate moment. Although the shaman was perfectly aware that he was at times merely performing tricks, he nevertheless was firmly convinced of his power to deal with spirits. When he fell into a trance, it was a real trance; when he had a fit, it was a real fit. He regarded his ultimate purpose as an honest one, and if he could intensify the supernatural experience by slightly hoodwinking his audience, then he went ahead and hoodwinked them. So convinced of their own efficacy were the shamans that when they themselves were sick in spirit they called in a fellow practitioner to administer treatment.

The life of the Eskimo was hedged in by numerous taboos that appear ridiculous to us and that would seem to have handicapped the Eskimo in his struggle for survival. One taboo, for instance, prohibited any work during a time of mourning; so if someone died during the long winter of privation, hunger invariably resulted. Another taboo prohibited using whaling tools for more than one season, despite the scarcity of raw materials. Such prohibitions appear to run counter to the best interests of the Eskimo. Was there some hidden value in these ridiculous taboos, or did the Eskimo manage to survive despite them?

No doubt many of the Eskimo's religious observances worked to his detriment. Yet they continued to be observed because they afforded certain social benefits that could not be achieved by other methods, although the Eskimo himself undoubtedly had no conscious understanding of these benefits. Note that all the taboos were concerned with rather ridiculous matters, and they were all very demanding, just as the hazing of freshmen on some college campuses demands careful observance of trivial customs. Actually taboos had much the same result as hazing. They promoted cooperation because all the people were made to suffer together. In the simple society of the Eskimo, the sharing of fears and the scrupulous attention to details of conduct created a social bond. The Eskimo's compliance with folkways, no matter how seemingly foolish, afforded him a better unifying social mechanism than he probably could have devised rationally.

Today the primeval life of the Eskimo has changed, for the whites brought him a technology that resulted in new relationships to the environment and to other bands. Commercial fishing encouraged small Eskimo groups to merge into large villages. The Eskimo now imports canned and preserved foods from the temperate and tropic zones to help him through the winter. He has switched to a cash-and-credit economy: nowadays he earns money by working at a fish-canning factory or by turning out soapstone carvings for tourists. Yet despite these changes in his way of life, the Eskimo, the first of the native Americans to encounter whites, has managed to salvage more of his culture than any other aboriginal group in North America.

Mr. Farb, curator of American Indian cultures at the Riverside Museum in New York City and a consultant to the Smithsonian Institution, is an anthropologist and historian. He is also a prolific writer; the book from which this article is excerpted is his twelfth. Entitled MAN'S RISE TO CIVILIZATION AS SHOWN BY THE INDIANS OF NORTH AMERICA FROM PRIMEVAL TIMES TO THE COMING OF THE INDUSTRIAL STATE, *the book will be published this month by E. P. Dutton & Co., Inc., and will be a November selection of the Book-of-the-Month Club.*

WHEN THE HURRICANE STRUCK

CONTINUED FROM PAGE 39

sure the Gulf was harmless. And some people simply never received any warning. By seven o'clock most Galvestonians were awake. Many had, in fact, already finished breakfast and were preparing for a full Saturday's work; in 1900 the six-day week was routine. Many residents near the beach, however, stopped long enough to watch the tremendous display put on by the giant waves. It was a grand sight, they agreed, and the word began to spread across the city. Other citizens hurriedly dressed for wet weather and came to view the spectacle, arriving by horse and buggy, by streetcar, on foot. They watched, entranced, while enormous waves demolished amusement houses, a bathhouse, and piers.

At least one youngster viewed the scene with alarm—King Vidor, who later became a motion-picture director. Long afterward, he recalled that moment:

As we looked up the sandy street the mile to the sea I could see the waves crash against the streetcar trestle then shoot into the air as high as the telephone poles. Higher. My mother didn't speak as we watched three or four waves.

I was only six years old then but I remember now that it seemed as if we were in a bowl looking up toward the level of the sea and as we stood there in the sandy street, my mother and I, I wanted to take my mother's hand and hurry her away. I felt as if the sea was going to break over the edge of the bowl and come pouring down upon us.

The tide continued to rise during the rest of the morning. The water, encroaching from Galveston Bay to the north (forced ashore on the bay side by the prevailing winds), was coming in even larger volume from the Gulf side, where the waves were growing ever more tremendous. In the low areas of the city, water quickly covered the streets. The inexorable tide—and a rising, whipping wind—soon forced most of the curious at the beach to seek shelter.

At 10:00 A.M. Joseph Cline, at the Weather Bureau, received a telegraph order to change the storm warning from northwest to northeast. Hoisted within five minutes, the flag was soon ripped apart by the wind. Later the flagstaff itself was destroyed. The significance was not lost; the city might be on the storm's immediate right after all.

During the morning the wind in Galveston had been mostly from the north, varying from northwest to northeast, and any weatherman could realize that it would come later from the east, southeast, and south, that being the pattern for a tropical hurricane. And when the wind went to the east and southeast it seemed likely to throw the Gulf over Galveston Island. By noon the Gulf had crept halfway across the city in some places, and had submerged the two causeways linking the island with the mainland.

At 2:30 in the afternoon Joseph went up to the Levy Building's roof. He found that the rain gauge had blown away. The last reading was 1.27 inches, but the Weather Bureau later estimated that a total of ten inches fell during the storm period. He had completed the rest of a special observation, to be telegraphed to Washington, and had returned to the third-floor office when Isaac, still warning people on the south side of the island, stopped long enough to telephone. He had realized by this time that "an awful disaster" was upon the city. He told his brother, "Half the city is under water." Then he relayed some additional information for the central office, stressing the need for relief.

Joseph added his brother's information to his own report and left for the Western Union telegraph office to dispatch it. He waded through the business section, through water swirling knee-deep in places, picking his way among floating wooden pavement blocks. When he reached the Western Union office he learned that the wires had been down for two hours.

He went to the Postal Telegraph office, a few doors beyond; its wires were also down. He struggled back to the weather office.

He finally managed to get a telephone call through to the Western Union office in Houston. Just as he finished reading his message, the telephone wire snapped, leaving Galveston isolated from the world.

Joseph then left the office in John Blagden's care and struck out for the beach area to help his brother. Again he struggled through flooded streets, while gusts of wind frequently blew him off his course. Along the way he shouted warnings that the worst of the storm was still ahead. When he could not make his voice heard above the wind he pointed to the center of the city, urging people to go there.

Still, many residents stayed put. Some were confident that their houses could weather even this storm; and by now they had also realized that venturing out had become too dangerous. Slate sharp enough to decapitate a man was flying about, carried by a wind approaching one hundred miles per hour; bricks, lumber, and pieces of metal were raining down.

From late afternoon on, many residents were literally caught in a trap. Those in beachfront houses had delayed too long, but now they were afraid to leave.

At 5:15, while Joseph was nearing his brother's residence, the wind gauge atop the Levy Building whirled to pieces. The last recorded velocity was eighty-four miles per hour, but the wind was gusting to at least one hundred. Isaac later estimated a velocity of "110 or 120 miles an hour"; some guesses went higher.

Joseph climbed the steps to his brother's front porch. He motioned to several persons across the street to go into town; then he entered the house. His brother was already there, along with nearly fifty neighbors.

Joseph's first concern, typically, was for his job. He reported to his brother that the barometer had dropped below twenty-nine inches. But when Isaac advised him to take the horse and return to the office, he refused. His usefulness there had ended, he had concluded; perhaps here he could be of some assistance.

Downtown, from Saint Mary's Cathedral, the Angelus rang out in the six o'clock gloom. To Father James M. Kirwin, the pastor, it sounded like "a warning of death and destruction." Suddenly the cathedral towers swayed. The two-ton bell was torn from its iron bands and clasps, and crashed to the floor. The Right Reverend Nicholas Gallagher, bishop of the diocese of Galveston, turned to Father Kirwin, gestured toward several other clergymen waiting in the room, and said, "Prepare these priests for death."

Nearer the Gulf, the eastern and western portions of the city were being swept away. Roaring seas smashed houses to debris and hurled the wreckage against structures farther inland. Most survivors said that by the time the storm reached its peak they held out no hope of living through it. They watched as brick buildings were flattened by the undermining action of the water, and as victims were cut, bruised, or killed by debris. Worst of all, they heard their own buildings creak and groan. Most had resigned themselves to dying. They hoped it would happen quickly.

In one house near the beach a group of fifty hovered in a second-floor bedroom. Above the ceaseless din of the storm several of them heard a little girl's voice ask, "Mamma, how can I drown?"

For her and for hundreds of other Galvestonians, the answer came just after six. A four-foot storm wave, sweeping ashore ahead of the hurricane's vortex, crashed over Galveston Island, destroying many of the buildings yet standing.

About six blocks east of the Cline residence, Clarence Howth, an attorney, realized the effects of the wave. A new father, Howth was understandably concerned about the welfare of his wife and their hours-old baby. With them were Mrs. Howth's father, Dr. John B. Sawyer, her brother, a nurse, and a maid.

When the water rose almost to their second-floor bedroom Howth supervised the transfer of his wife and child up the steep stairs to the attic. Soon the salt spray was coming in the attic window.

Mrs. Howth called to her father, "Papa, are we going to die?"

"No, daughter," he answered. "It's almost over now." Within minutes the house collapsed.

"The crash threw me away from my wife, and I sank underneath the water," Howth recounted. He struggled to the surface, grabbed a window frame, and clung to it while he was carried out into the Gulf and back again. Like many other Galvestonians, he had lost his family, his house—everything but his life.

Shortly before the storm wave struck, Isaac Cline had opened the front door a crack to watch the weather. While he was peering outside, the sudden rise of four feet sent water above his waist before he could move. The Gulf, now ten feet deep around his home, had reached a record tidal level of 15.2 feet. One hour later, the Cline residence stood alone; all nearby houses were gone.

The people in the Cline house were crowded into a second-floor room on the windward side; the Clines had reasoned that if the house were blown over, they would be on the top wall as it fell. Joseph warned them that collapse was imminent. Indeed, they heard and saw wreckage from other buildings crashing against the house; by 7:30 both the front and rear porches had been sliced off. Then they observed, bearing down upon them, a great piece of wreckage from what had been a streetcar trestle. Rails still held it together—it was a two-hundred-foot-long battering ram powered by more energy than man could ever hope to generate. As the trestle moved, it gathered random wreckage. It upset one raft carrying twenty-five persons and swept on toward the Cline house.

Some of the crowd became panicky. Many had begun to sing, in a prideful effort to discipline themselves, but others surrendered to hysteria. At impact, they felt the house shudder and move; it was afloat. The wind caught it and forced it into a slow forward roll; but before it capsized, Joseph grabbed the hands of two of his nieces and lunged backward through the window. He smashed through the glass and the storm shutters, and the momentum carried all three through the opening. The house rolled over, and then bobbed to the surface. Joseph and the two youngsters found themselves alone on the top side, clinging to the outside wall. To their knowledge no one else had survived. Rain drenched them, but they saw that the clouds had begun to break. They even had an occasional glimpse of the moon.

Joseph, remembering that drowning persons will seize any object within reach, crawled to the broken window and yelled "Come here! Come here!" into the darkness below. Then he lowered his legs through the opening and swung them back and forth in the water. There was no response.

The wall on which they crouched began to pitch. Under the pounding their insecure refuge was slowly breaking up.

Nearby, but unseen, Isaac and his youngest daughter were clinging to floating debris. He had seen his brother break through the window; but then a dresser had skidded across the room and pinned him and his wife and the daughter against a mantel. All three had been carried under water, and Isaac was certain he would drown. Despairing, he decided to take water into his lungs, and when he did blackness engulfed him.

But he regained consciousness. He realized that his head was above water and that several large, bobbing timbers were brushing against his chest. Nearby he saw his daughter, on a shattered piece of the roof, trying to raise herself, but a plank across her back held her down. He regained his senses in time to see a board careening toward her; he raised his hand and deflected it. Then he groped in the debris-littered water for his wife, but he could not find her.

Isaac crawled onto the piece of roof that held his daughter and took her in his arms. A few minutes later he discerned three human shapes bent low on pitching debris, about a hundred feet to windward.

"Who's there?" he shouted into the storm. One of his daughters called back, "Who are you?" The Cline family were reunited about half an hour after the house had fallen—all but Mrs. Cline, of whom there was no sign.

They were forced to keep moving from one sinking piece of debris to another. At one time a floating house bore down upon them, but just before it struck, the two men grabbed for its top; their weight was enough to pull the top far enough down for all of them to scramble onto it. They huddled there for three hours.

Occasionally one of them would be knocked off the "raft" and would have to fight his way back through the water. Once, while drifting toward the city again, they heard cries from the second-story window of a house in their path. But they were helpless: their raft

This drawing, from an early book on the disaster, shows a Galveston street relatively untouched by the hurricane.

rammed into the house, and Isaac was hit by some falling timber. Luckily, he was not badly hurt.

At one point Joseph noticed a small girl struggling in the water—his youngest niece, he assumed, knocked off the raft. He grabbed for her dress and pulled her out. Several minutes passed before he realized that all three of his nieces had been accounted for and that this girl was a stranger.

The storm had begun to diminish noticeably. Bright moonlight occasionally illuminated the ghastly scene of destruction, and the southerly wind had rather suddenly become almost gentle. The five Clines and the young stranger felt their raft plow into other wreckage; it shuddered and stopped. They were "aground" in the midst of debris piled fifteen and twenty feet high.

They saw, about fifty yards away, a two-story house poking above the wreckage and decided that it offered the most immediate haven. Joseph went first, gingerly picking his way across the debris for a few feet, then turning and taking the children from his brother, who lifted them to him one by one. Thus they finally reached the house, where the occupants pulled them in through a second-floor window. They were amazed to find themselves only a few blocks from where their own house had stood.

By ten that night the storm was well past; the center had moved inland a few miles to the southwest of the city. The south wind, though now comparatively slight, pushed some of the water in the northern section of Galveston back into the bay. The area to the south, however, was not so fortunate. There the same wind tended to hold the flood on the island, and a line of debris several blocks inland, acting as a dam, also kept the water from flowing back into the Gulf.

An eerie stillness settled over Galveston as the water and wind relinquished their hold. Occasionally the dreadful quiet was broken by the cry of someone buried beyond help in the debris. But the cries soon ceased, and weeks—months—were required to recover the victims. The body of Isaac Cline's wife was not located until October 3—under the very wreckage on which her family had drifted until it went aground. Many victims could not be identified. Others—and there were hundreds—were never found; they had simply vanished in a storm that took between six and eight thousand lives and cost seventeen million dollars in property damage. It was the worst recorded natural disaster that has befallen North America.

The catastrophe was so great that some Galvestonians were quite willing to abandon their city; but most residents at once involved themselves in rebuilding.

The recovery was astounding. The city built a sea wall seventeen feet above mean low tide, and over a foot above the 1900 storm level. Finished in 1904, the wall was put to the test eleven years later, when another hurricane and a fourteen-foot tide assaulted the city. Property damage was less than five million dollars—and only twelve lives were lost.

Galveston raised its ground level by as much as seventeen feet by pumping in sand from the floor of the Gulf. The process necessitated first raising buildings, telephone poles, streetcar tracks, and shrubbery; the heaviest building raised weighed three thousand tons.

A short time after the 1900 hurricane Galveston devised the city commission form of government. Its previous format—a mayor and twelve aldermen—had long been fiscally unsatisfactory and had been unable to cope with various specific duties in digging out from the storm. The city commission idea soon spread to other municipalities across the country. (In 1961 Galveston again switched its type of government, this time to the council-city manager format.)

Before the storm a favorite topic of conversation in Galveston had been the new century, and particularly the date it would begin. The Vatican, among other world authorities, had declared it would start January 1, 1901, and predominantly Catholic Galveston largely accepted this, although a few insisted the actual date was January 1, 1900. But the nineteenth century actually came to an abrupt end for the island city on September 8, 1900. Nowhere else was the changing of the centuries more noticeable, for the lives of virtually all Galvestonians had been vitally affected.

Clarence Howth, one of those to whom the storm had granted a grudging stay of execution, is a case in point. Two weeks after the hurricane he visited the lot near the beach where his home had stood—where, on the Friday night before the storm, he had been watering cauliflower plants in his back yard; it was just hours before he had become a father. Now there was only a torn piece of garden hose attached to a water pipe to mark the site.

"It seemed as a dream," he mused, "of a thing that had never been."

Mr. Weems is a member of the English department at Baylor University in Waco, Texas. He wrote A Weekend in September *(Holt, 1957), a fuller treatment of the Galveston hurricane, and contributed "Peary or Cook: Who Discovered the North Pole?" to our April, 1962, issue.*

The Erie Canal Passed This Way

CONTINUED FROM PAGE 30

around 1910, thanks to its conversion for use as a road bridge. And a second and larger aqueduct erected at Rexford about 1840 to carry an enlarged canal stood until just last year, also because it was converted to a highway bridge.

Another major aqueduct crossed the Genesee River in the west, where the new village of Rochester was mushrooming. The Genesee was a turbulent river, and the aqueduct piers had to be sunk into the solid rock of the river bottom. The entire structure was bolted and bound with iron into a unit 802 feet long; it had eleven stone arches, nine of them fifty feet across. Not far east of Rochester the canal was forced to cross the deep valley of Irondequoit Creek. Initial plans were to build a wooden aqueduct sixty feet high and a quarter of a mile long, and then, once the canal was operating, to bring in earth by boats and dump it from this structure to build a permanent base. But fears that a wooden trestle could not withstand high winds caused the engineers to substitute an embankment of stone and earth, with Irondequoit Creek carried through a culvert beneath it. In this day of earth-fill dams, superhighway interchanges, and other massive works constructed with huge earth-moving machines, we tend to grow blasé about such engineering projects. But at Irondequoit Creek the only earth-moving machines available for creating a small mountain ridge were horse-drawn scrapers and wagons, and men with shovels. Sweat is a more old-fashioned moving force than gasoline and diesel fuel, but it served the nation well for a long time.

At the Cayuga Marshes the canal was dug under water six inches or a foot deep, but it was not the engineering problems of digging a ditch and raising a towpath in semiliquid muck that gave trouble. The swamps swarmed with mosquitoes, among them the genus *Anopheles*, carrier of malaria, which laid low entire work crews until cold weather came.

The supreme engineering accomplishment of the western portion was the three-mile cut through solid rock some twenty miles northeast of Buffalo. To raise the canal sixty-six feet up a steep rock face, a double set of five locks was blasted out. Everywhere else on the canal there were only single locks, and east- and westbound traffic took turns going through. But at Lockport (as the town that sprang up at the site was named) the locks were doubled, to avoid traffic tie-ups.

Not all the streams that crossed Clinton's Ditch were bridged by aqueducts; on a number of the smaller ones a bridge was built only for the tow teams. The stream was dammed below the canal crossing to create a more or less placid pool, and guard locks were built where the canal entered the stream, to prevent the canal's being flooded in times of high water. A boat was locked into the stream, was towed across, and re-entered the canal through the guard lock on the opposite side.

There was a great deal more to the canal than met the eye. It was laid out so that there were streams or lakes to supply water for operating locks and to replace evaporation and leakage. The feeders bringing in this water required an elaborate system of gates and sluices, and formed a great network of small branch canals on which farmers could bring their butter and bacon by skiff to the Erie. There were waste weirs to discharge excess water in times of flood; there were culverts and fences; there were more than three hundred bridges that had to be built where the canal cut farmers' lands in two; and there were weighlocks to weigh canal boats at principal ports to determine toll charges.

Clinton's Ditch prospered. Eastern goods and a stream of emigrants with their belongings travelled west, while Great Lakes vessels carried the produce of the Middle West to Buffalo for transfer to east-bound canal boats. Western New York, which had been almost a wilderness, filled with farmers, and a string of towns burgeoned all along the canal.

In 1835, only ten years after the Erie's completion, the commissioners recommended that it be enlarged to handle bigger boats and more traffic. A program was shortly begun to widen the channel to seventy feet and deepen it to seven feet; the locks were to be doubled to handle two-way traffic, as at Lockport, and increased

BOTH: *Harper's New Monthly Magazine*, DECEMBER, 1873

Steering a canalboat required more skill than the lackadaisical pose of this helmsman indicates; bringing the clumsy craft into a lock with only inches to spare required competence and a steady hand and eye, no job for the ever-drunk Erie canalman of legend.

considerably in size. A number of streams across which Clinton's Ditch had passed its boats at water level were bridged by aqueducts on the Enlarged Erie, as the modernized canal was known, and existing aqueducts were rebuilt. Some of these structures still stand—at least in part—their massive romanesque arches indicating that the planners had every confidence that the Erie would go on for many generations.

The enlargement program moved by fits and starts, tied to canal revenues, and was not finally completed until 1862, when heavy wartime shipping brought large toll collections. But by then an unforeseen cloud was rising over the future of the canal. The Mohawk and Hudson Railroad began operating out of Albany in 1831, and though it and subsequent railroads along the Erie were first complacently viewed as short-line passenger carriers, an awakening came when eight lines joined in 1842 to connect Albany and Buffalo by rail, a union that eleven years later became the New York Central. At first the railroads were not permitted to haul freight except when the Erie was closed in winter, and even then they were forced to pay canal tolls on what they carried; but this restriction was removed in 1851, and the rail lines became full competitors.

During the heyday of the Erie, connecting canals laced the state. A waterway was completed to Oswego on Lake Ontario in 1828, finally accomplishing what the old Western Inland Lock Navigation Company had attempted in the 1790's. Cayuga Lake and Seneca Lake were tied to the Erie; the Genesee Valley Canal provided a link to the Allegheny River and thus to the Ohio; the Chenango Canal extended southwestward from Utica on the Erie as far as Binghamton; and the Chemung Canal, running south from Seneca Lake, linked up at the state border to a branch of the extensive Pennsylvania canal system. Most fantastic was the Black River Canal, connecting the Erie at Rome with the Black River to the north; it required 108 locks in only thirty-five miles. By 1877 the state began disposing of some of these lateral canals, which by then had long since outlived their usefulness.

As early as 1869 the tonnage carried by the New York Central and Erie railroads exceeded what went down the canal. A halving of canal tolls had not helped much, and in 1882 the voters, by constitutional amendment, made the Erie a free canal. But it continued to decline and by 1898 was almost in a state of collapse. In 1903 a plan to turn it into a barge canal was approved.

The work was completed in 1918. The towpath was gone; boats henceforth went through pushed by a tug. The minimum bottom width of the channel was now seventy-five feet, the depth twelve feet, and, because the terminals were at Waterford and Tonawanda instead of Albany and Buffalo, the canal was shorter. It is now 338 miles long and has only thirty-five locks, with lifts running as high as forty feet (the highest lock in Clinton's Ditch was a little over a dozen feet). Most of the middle and eastern parts of the waterway were relocated, sometimes by many miles. The rocky Mohawk, shunned by the two old Eries, is made part of the Barge Canal by a series of dams and locks that tame its turbulence. The Champlain Canal, the Oswego Canal to Lake Ontario, and the canal to Cayuga and Seneca lakes were also retained and modernized.

Great parts of the Enlarged Erie were left abandoned far from the Barge Canal, and there they wait for the antiquarian and historian to visit them, as well as for the wrecking crew to come. Many of the old aqueducts have been at least partially destroyed. Massive and built to last, they are nevertheless no match for the wrecking ball and the bulldozer. Sometimes the central arches and piers were knocked out, either to prevent ice from piling up against them during the spring break-up, or to permit passage of the Barge Canal, which in places was rerouted into the streams. Without a center, even the best of aqueducts loses some of its aesthetic appeal.

Some abandoned segments of the Erie canals, being state property, were put to other state uses—as the right of way of a highway, for example. But well over half the total still lie empty and unused, silent reminders of the past. Not all of them are forgotten in distant fields and pastures: the old lock at Pittsford, for one, stands behind a shopping center, easy to see and easy to reach. Other locks and structures are almost as handy, or are being made so: a group of junior historians at Jordan, for instance, has cleared the land around the old lock there in something of a do-it-yourself restoration movement.

The canal has often left a stamp even where it has disappeared. Erie Boulevards in Syracuse, Schenectady, Utica, Rome, and possibly other New York communities were not named accidentally; they were the routes the old Erie followed through those towns. But other historic spots have disappeared without trace; Lock Number One at Albany, which separated the early Erie canals from the Hudson River, is now somewhere under a truck parking lot.

Canal history buffs, an unusually dedicated band, have been able to preserve relics of the old canals, sometimes against considerable odds; and in at least one case they have won the co-operation of the highway people, a group often accused of being completely indifferent to historic values. When a state highway route was planned on the line of the old Black River Canal, it was designed so as to bypass and preserve an especially impressive flight of four locks, and picnic facilities and a lookout point are planned to make a small park of the area. Though other locks of the old canal are scheduled for destruction in the same operation, canal historians, who realize that not everything can be saved, are happy with the arrangement.

The matter of period restoration is something else again. There are certain problems of economics involved, and, in the absence of heavy financial support from some charitable foundation, any project to give the public a picture of the old canal in action may have difficulties. Rome, where digging of the Erie be-

There were large canalboat terminals in New York Harbor, among them the basin in Brooklyn pictured here. The boats were towed up the Hudson River to the Erie Canal at Albany, twenty or thirty of them behind a single steamboat.

gan, is restoring a two-mile section of the Enlarged Erie, along which two canal boats, built according to old plans and pulled by real horses on the towpath, will carry tourists. But this is one of the points where economics lays a chill hand on the enterprise. It has been found that the canal boats, which could be built for $3,500 each during the days of the towpath canal, will cost a total of $117,000 to reproduce today. It will take a good many tourist dollars to make Rome's project break even.

Thus, the ramifications of preserving or reconstructing historical sites are complex, especially when the sites are elongated in a thin ribbon for miles. It may be that the problem will be compounded for a coming generation. There is talk about modernizing the present Barge Canal, and if this comes about, sections of it will probably be bypassed and abandoned, and their preservation may some day be an issue. However, the Barge Canal is a placid waterway; its traffic is modest and it can make little claim to being the gateway to the West. Though there is an increasing number of pleasure boats on the canal, many hours can sometimes pass without a vessel going through, while the huge motor transports and tanker trucks roar by, often within hearing distance, on the Thomas E. Dewey Thruway. Who knows what nostalgic highway buff not too long hence will be fighting to preserve for posterity one of the more gracefully tangled interchanges of that thruway?

Mr. Andrist, an editor in the American Heritage book division, is the author of The Erie Canal *(American Heritage Junior Library, 1964) and of* The Long Death: The Last Days of the Plains Indian *(Macmillan, 1964).*

"A CHASE UP INTO THE SKY"

CONTINUED FROM PAGE 20

FM radio antenna was installed just below the television facility.) The red warning lights along the television spire are the only ones that operate 365 nights a year. Since the mid-fifties the others—the floodlights for the top thirty stories and the massive fluorescent panels of the tower—have been extinguished on cloudy or foggy nights during the wild-fowl migratory seasons. It was found that cloud-diffused light tended to disorient birds and to lure them into fatal collisions with the building.

The Empire State Building cost just under 41 million dollars, including land; in 1951, the year after John J. Raskob died, a group headed by Roger L. Stevens bought the building for 34 million dollars. The Prudential Insurance Company of America bought the land for another 17 million dollars and set up a lease-back arrangement with the new owners. In 1954 a Chicago syndicate led by Colonel Henry Crown acquired the Empire State for 51.5 million dollars. The most recent ownership change came in 1961: Prudential, together with a syndicate headed by Lawrence Wien, a lawyer, and Harry Helmsley, a realtor, bought the building for 65 million dollars. Prudential became the owner of record, and granted the Helmsley-Wien syndicate a 114-year master lease. They pay an annual rent of 3.2 million dollars while collecting some 14 million dollars from tenants, TV networks, and tourists who come to see the city from the sky.

The past few years have been good to Empire State. With about 932 tenants, it is all but full to capacity. Two sub-ground-level floors, unoccupied since construction, have recently been opened up, adding another 75,000 square feet of space. As always, there is a staggering variety of goods and services available within the building.

But ownership of the capsule metropolis carries with it many headaches and means a ceaseless battle against obsolescence. The elevators have been automated, and air conditioning has been installed. The exterior has already been cleaned and recoated, and the window frames have been repainted. The maintenance cost is a sizable 1.35 million dollars per year.

As New York buildings go, the Empire State is no longer young; at thirty-seven, it is older than the Waldorf-Astoria was when it was knocked down in "the march of progress." The great post-World War II building boom has provided New York with a great many newer and shinier structures, all equipped with the latest competitive advantages. Currently there is an enormous demand for office space, and the Empire State prospers; but at the next ebb of the economic tide it may not be the last to find itself unfilled.

Even more ominous is the prospect, at last, of a taller building. The projected downtown World Trade Center proposes to shoot two towers—each 10,000 feet square—1,350 feet into the sky. Should the Trade Center take over as the site of television transmission—and the distinct possibility exists not because of its height but because of its greater roominess at the top—Empire State will have lost the glorious title of the world's tallest building. It will have taken its place, however reluctantly, as the latest in a long line of has-beens. The day of its reign will have ended—but what a day it was.

Frances Low, wife of New York City Councilman Robert Low, is a freelance writer living in New York. Among her sources for this article was Empire State, A Pictorial Record of Its Construction, *by Vernon H. Bailey (W. E. Rudge, 1931). For further reading on Lewis Hine: Judith Mara Gutman's* Lewis Hine and the American Social Conscience *(Walker, 1967).*

Grant and the Politicians CONTINUED FROM PAGE 35

This bears all the earmarks of a deal that is a little too clever. The Blairs often promised more than they could deliver, and Weed was not the only high Republican to fall into a panic this summer. That Lincoln himself took any stock in this gambit is doubtful. But he knew about it, and he would not have put McClellan's name on the agenda if he had not intended to discuss the matter with Grant.

And there it was. Grant could not make a routine military appointment without reflecting on the presidential election; indeed, the political tide was so strong and so confusing that routine military acts all became extraordinary, as if something great had to be fought out in men's minds before anyone could act on the battlefield.

A peace movement was going on, and General Meade remarked that "the camp is full of rumors and reports of many kinds" as a result. The movement was largely the creation of Horace Greeley, the hard-war abolitionist editor of the New York *Tribune,* who occasionally carried a pundit's eccentricity to excess and who now had gone off on a tangent. Greeley somehow had got in touch with Confederate agents in Canada and had absorbed the idea that Lincoln could end the war if he would just sit down and talk reasonably with reasonable Confederates about a peace that would be honorable and satisfying to both sides. Greeley wrote despairingly to Lincoln about "our bleeding, bankrupt, almost dying country"; he failed to realize that the only peace Richmond wanted was one that saved both southern independence and southern slavery . . . and unfortunately he did not know that the Confederates in Canada had no authorization to talk to Lincoln about anything. Lincoln called his bluff, giving Greeley full power to bring the supposed Confederate emissaries to the White House; Greeley finally learned that he had been talking to the wrong people and went away sorrowing, aware that he had been had and feeling that the President had been too stiff-necked. It all came to nothing, but it was one of the things that had to be thought about when the military campaign was up for discussion.

Another was the state of mind of the Republican Radicals—the real Radicals, harder and less eccentric than Greeley: the people the Blairs wanted to beat. Lincoln had just applied a pocket veto to the Wade-Davis Bill, in which Senator Ben Wade of Ohio and Congressman Henry Winter Davis of Maryland, Radicals who burned with an undying flame, had persuaded Congress to lay down stern terms for the eventual restoration of the Union. (It would never be restored on anybody's terms until somebody got Jubal Early away from the Potomac, but the point was not raised.) Lincoln announced that the measure would never become law with his consent, but remarked that any repentant southern state that wanted to come back into the Union on the Wade-Davis terms could do so, and all of this put the bill's authors into a great fury. On August 5 they issued a formal manifesto, attacking Lincoln with unmeasured venom. What they and their followers would have said if McClellan had been restored to a high military command just then goes beyond the reach of any normal imagination. Anyway, here was another point to consider.

Which brought to mind, inevitably, General Butler. Nobody really knew what Butler was up to—to this day, nobody really knows—but he was a hard-war man, a Democrat, and a politician with a solid following back home, and the situation offered possibilities. General Patrick noted that Butler visited Meade on July 20, and wrote: "He has been offered the Chicago nomination and is playing everyone to get some power over each individual." Nobody had actually "offered" Butler anything, but anything could happen, and if he went off the reservation he could almost certainly keep Lincoln from being re-elected. His chief of staff, Colonel John W. Shaffer, went to New York to take soundings, and on August 17 he wrote to Butler assuring him that "the country has gone to hell unless Mr. Lincoln can be beat by a good loyal man."

Shaffer's analysis offers a picture of the frenzy that had come upon the political scene. If the Democrats nominated a peace man, said Shaffer, the Republican leaders felt that the Republicans ought to have a new convention and name a candidate other than Lincoln, who was both too warlike for the peaceminded and too lacking in grimness for the warlike. Shaffer said that Thurlow Weed "thinks Lincoln can be prevailed upon to draw off," and he added that the same feeling had been expressed by Leonard Swett of Illinois, one of the group that had rammed Lincoln's nomination through the 1860 convention. The leading Republicans, as Shaffer sized things up, agreed that Lincoln must withdraw as soon as the Democratic convention was over: "Nearly all speak of you as the man"— remember, this letter was addressed to Butler—"but I studiously avoid bringing your name in." The most that could be expected of Lincoln, Shaffer concluded, was that he would help keep other men from running, thereby preserving a clear path for Butler. . . . If someone, somewhere, had quietly dangled a carrot in front of General Butler's nose, it can only be said that this was that kind of summer.

It was that kind of summer. Everything interlocked; the Army of the Potomac, having been built to a political pattern, reflected the doubt and suspicion that politics had created, so that failure was fated. On July 26, four days before the Battle of the Crater—an attempt, organized under General Ambrose Burnside, to tunnel beneath the Confederate defense works at Petersburg and explode a great quantity of powder, thereby blasting open a path to Richmond—General Patrick had a long talk with Meade and foresaw disaster because of "the jealousy on the part of Corps Commanders against each other & against Meade—especially the bad blood that exists between Meade & Burnside—preventing unanimity of counsels, or concert of action, even among the troops belonging to the Army of the Potomac." Patrick went on to say: "The same spirit alluded to . . . so hostile to Burnside will prevent Meade, probably, from taking hold with any vim to carry out Burnside's idea of an assault following the explosion of his mine; which if a successful 'Blow up' as it seems to me can be followed up by an assault which will carry everything before it." Patrick believed after this chat that both Grant and his advisers recognized "the feeling in the North & East that Grant has failed in this campaign" and said that the administration was looking for a scapegoat.

Patrick, to be sure, was a gossip-monger, but the feeling he detected was caught by others. An army surgeon, Dr. John H. Brinton, who had known Grant from the old days at Cairo and now was on duty around Washington, wrote at this time that Grant "had not many friends amongst the Army of the Potomac men. They were all McClellan men, and insisted that Grant was only treading the same path followed by McClellan and that his bloody victories were fruitless. They did not like him and had no confidence in him. The Northern people as a mass believed in him; the Eastern, especially the troops of the Army of the Potomac, did not." Congressman James Ashley of Ohio warned a Grant aide in mid-July that having visited the army he found "a good deal of discontent and mutinous spirit among staff officers of the Army of the Potomac," and said that "a good deal of McClellanism . . . was manifested."

The feeling of a certain part of the officer corps was summed up by Lieutenant Colonel Carswell McClellan, who had served on General Humphrey's staff up to the opening of this campaign. Grant, said Colonel McClellan, just did not understand the Army of the Potomac: "The army was composed of citizens of our entire Union—men of the North and South, and East and West, stood side by side in its ranks and led its columns. The conquering of 'sectional feeling' was the very duty that had called out and created, from an untrained mass of patriots, an army of loyal veterans—'the grandest army gathered on this continent, at all times true to its commander-in-chief, whoever it might be.' There was no vain boasting in the grim story written all along the way from the James river up to Gettysburg"—that is, in the army's story in the days before Grant—and although the soldiers did have prejudices, they were loyal to the Union, "however blind they may have been to the personal identity of 'that Western man' with the cause for which they fought."

Grant and Lincoln shared something, here. They were westerners, lacking in polish, unable to impress the cultivated easterners. Early in the war Lincoln's minister to Great Britain, Charles Francis Adams, had shuddered visibly when he went to the White House and actually saw the ungainly man who had appointed him and who had so little in common with the Adamses who had lived in the White House. This spring Richard Henry Dana, Jr., also of Massachusetts, had had a similar seizure when he first looked upon General Grant. The East had trouble adjusting itself to the fact that the rude West was dominant. Lincoln and Grant fitted each other perfectly, but to easterners they looked like a gawky, ill-chosen team.

Grant's people returned this antagonism, with interest added. Early in August, one of Grant's assistant adjutants general, Captain George K. Leet, wrote to the absent Colonel William R. Rowley: "My faith in the Army of the Potomac is gone, gone. . . ." A little later this summer General Grenville Dodge (the man who later built much of the railway to the Pacific) spent some time at headquarters recovering from a wound received in the fighting in front of Atlanta, and when he visited various corps and division commanders' tents "discovered a feeling that was a stranger to us in the West—a feeling, the existence of which seemed to me to bode no good." Everybody was criticizing either the Commanding General or some fellow officer, and Dodge said that although he had never heard this sort of talk in the western army, "I must say I heard it in the Army of the Potomac, and anything but kindly comments by one commander upon another, and as this was in the dark days of the war I had many misgivings about what I had heard." He talked about it with Grant's chief of staff, General John Rawlins, he said, and Rawlins laughed and replied: "General, this is not the old Army of the Tennessee."

It was not; which was one reason why some of the things Grant could do in his earlier days of fighting in the West could not quite be done here in the East. This army was too close to Washington, physically and spiritually, victimized by politics and at the same time contributing to the force that victimized it. Never for an instant could anyone forget—as it could be forgotten, now and then, in the West—that the army had been forged for use in a *civil* war and hence was as much subject to political pressure as the Post Office or the Treasury Department. This fact governed everything a commanding general did.

Except that once in a great while he could ignore it. In a way his chief responsibility was to recognize and use that once-in-a-while moment when it came.

When Grant had his talk with Lincoln at Fort Monroe, the command situation along the upper Potomac had become intolerable, and if a solution was not found at this meeting it had to be found immediately afterward. Grant no sooner got back to City Point on July 31 than he received a wire from Halleck saying that Jubal Early had gone north of the Potomac again and was on his way to Pennsylvania.

This was not entirely unexpected. Early had been edging forward into the lower part of the Shenandoah Valley for a week, occupying Martinsburg, sending cavalry squadrons across at Williamsport, Falling Waters, and Shepherdstown, and driving Yankee cavalry out of Hagerstown. Grant believed that although the Federal commanders had plenty of troops they were short of good cavalry, and on the day of the crater battle he ordered Meade to send a division of Sheridan's cavalry north at once.

Far from taking his main force over the river, Early was just sending cavalry north on a raid, but because this raid touched sensitive political nerves, the result might be as harmful to the Union cause as a major battle lost. Early's men believed they had a score to settle with the Yankees because Federal troops under Major General David Hunter had burned so many Virginia homes, and on July 30 a Rebel cavalry brigade led by General John McCausland cantered into Chambersburg, Pennsylvania, set fire to the place, and rode off to the west and south, leaving half of the town in ashes. This was in good Republican Pennsylvania with the presidential election only three months away, and if General Grant could not find someone to wage successful war along the Potomac, none of his other achievements was likely to mean very much.

On the night of the victory at Chattanooga there had been one general who wanted to press on until the last of the enemy's forces had been broken down and stamped on, and now Grant thought of him. On August 1 Grant told Meade he was going to send Phil Sheridan north, and he got off this telegram to Halleck:

I am sending General Sheridan for temporary duty whilst the enemy is being expelled from the border. Unless General Hunter is in the field in person, I want Sheridan put in command of all the troops in the field, with instructions to put himself south of the enemy and follow him to the death. Wherever the enemy goes let our troops go also. Once started up the Valley they ought to be followed until we get possession of the Virginia Central railroad. If General Hunter is in the field give Sheridan direct command of the Sixth Corps and cavalry division.

On the heels of this, Grant had Meade order the second of the army's three cavalry divisions to go north.

Neither Stanton nor Halleck approved of this appointment. Stanton thought Sheridan was altogether too young for such an important assignment, and when Sheridan got to Washington, his reception at the War Department was frosty. Halleck warned Grant that if Sheridan were placed in general command Hunter would ask to be relieved, and he added that if this did not happen it would be bad practice to make the VI Corps and the cavalry a separate command . . .

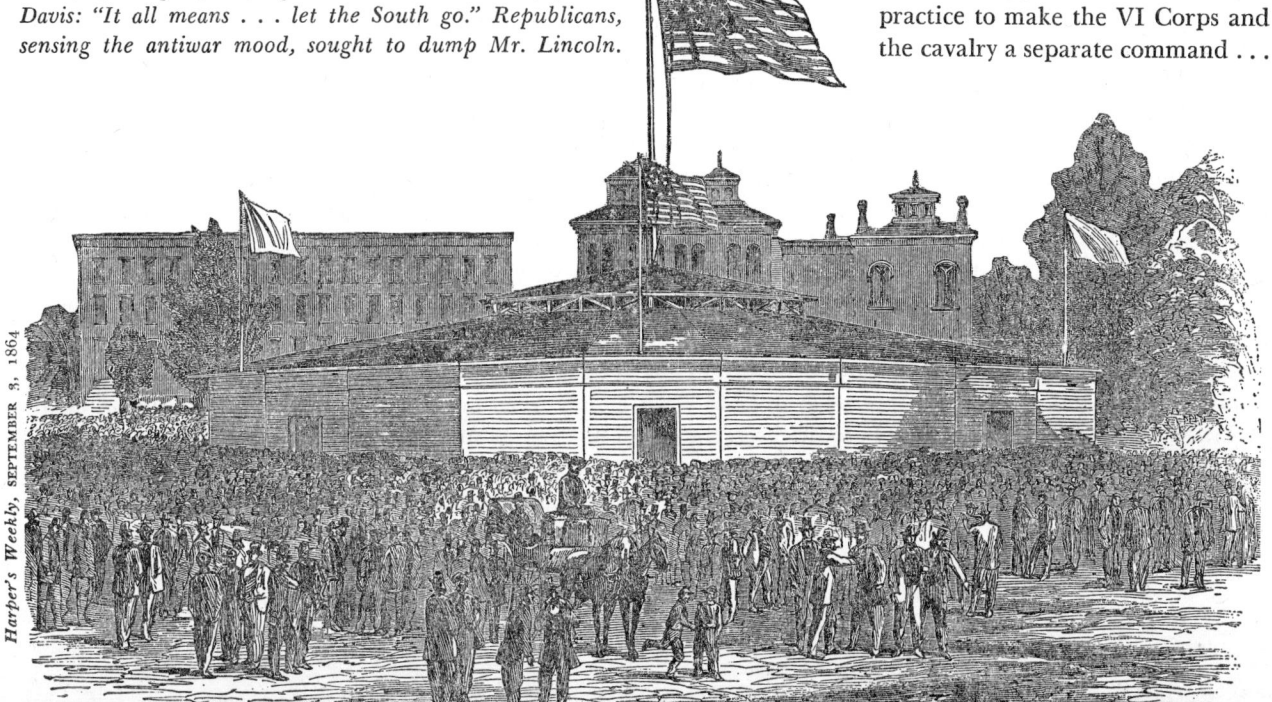

The Democratic convention opened in the "Wigwam" in Chicago on August 29, 1864. General McClellan was nominated; of the platform, a pro-Southerner wrote to Jefferson Davis: "It all means . . . let the South go." Republicans, sensing the antiwar mood, sought to dump Mr. Lincoln.

and altogether there was a good deal of clucking. Lincoln heard the clucking, and agreed that Sheridan was rather young; but under everything Lincoln also heard the hard ring of trumpets in Grant's order regarding Sheridan, and on August 3 he sent Grant a telegram:

I have seen your dispatch in which you say "I want Sheridan put in command of all the troops in the field, with instructions to put himself south of the enemy and follow him to the death. Wherever the enemy goes let our troops go also." This, I think, is exactly right as to how our forces should move, but please look over the dispatches you may have received from here even since you made that order, and discover, if you can, that there is any idea in the head of anyone here of "putting our army south of the enemy" or of "following him to the death" in any direction. I repeat to you it will neither be done nor attempted unless you watch it every day and hour and force it.

And now suddenly the great crisis of indecision and divided counsels was ended, and the fact that it had ended was as good as a victory. Grant that evening ordered a dispatch boat to get up steam for a quick voyage up the bay; he was on his way to the upper Potomac in less than two hours from the moment he got Lincoln's telegram, not to leave until the situation there had been arranged the way he wanted it.

Grant reached the Federal camp on the Monocacy River, forty miles northwest of Washington, on the evening of August 5. Awaiting him there, expecting nothing from him or from anyone else, were between 25,000 and 30,000 Federal soldiers—frustrated men drawn from three armies, sullenly awaiting the touch that would make a new army of them. Right now their only unity was a common knowledge that for the past month they had marched far and hard to no especial purpose. In command of them, and sharing to the full their awareness of wasted effort, was General Hunter, and when Grant that evening asked him where the enemy might be, General Hunter confessed that he had no idea. He said that he had received so many orders from the War Department recently, telling him to go from this place to that place, that he had lost all track of the people he was supposed to fight.

The one thing he knew was that Jubal Early's Confederates had not gone south. A little more than a week earlier they had driven Hunter's advance out of the lower Shenandoah Valley, and now they were believed to be arrayed somewhere near the Potomac, tying up the main line of the Baltimore & Ohio Railroad, sending cavalry raiders off into Pennsylvania, retaining command of the river crossings; full of evil intentions. The Federals on the Monocacy were protecting Washington faithfully enough, but they were not doing much of anything else.

Grant remarked that he would quickly find out where the Confederates were, and he ordered a general advance of the entire force to the hamlet of Halltown, south of the Potomac, four miles west of Harpers Ferry. Whatever General Early was doing, he was certain to respond to a Federal advance; Grant suspected correctly that as soon as Early heard of this move he would concentrate his own force somewhere near Martinsburg. If he tried to invade the North again, the army at Halltown would be ideally posted to get south of him (as Grant had prescribed) and follow him to the death. Having put the troops in motion—some of them took to the road that evening—Grant sat down to write out instructions governing their use.

Basically, these instructions were simple: find out where the enemy is and then go and get him. The Shenandoah Valley was to be taken away from Confederate use permanently, so that it could never again be an avenue for raiders or a granary for Lee's army, and the orders were grim:

In pushing up the Shenandoah Valley, as it is expected you will have to do first or last, it is desirable that nothing should be left to invite the enemy to return. Take all provisions, forage and stock wanted for the use of your command. Such as cannot be consumed, destroy. It is not desirable that the buildings should be destroyed—they should, rather, be protected; but the people should be informed that so long as an army can subsist among them recurrences of these raids must be expected, and we are determined to stop them at all hazards. . . .

The idea of laying waste the rich farming region of the valley so that it could no longer support Confederate armies or the Confederate capital had been formulated earlier. On July 14 Grant had written Halleck that when Early left Maryland he should be pursued up the valley by all available troops, who should be instructed to "eat out Virginia clear and clean as far as they go, so that crows flying over it for the balance of the season will have to carry their provender with them." This drew added point now from the fact that for a fortnight Early's troops had been actively helping to harvest crops in the lower valley, with details crossing the Potomac now and then to seize grain that the Maryland farmers had already harvested. All along, Early's expedition had been partly controlled by the needs of the Confederate commissary.

Having written out the orders, Grant went on to a more delicate matter. Hunter commanded the Department of West Virginia, and so all troops in that part of the country would be under him. But Sheridan was going to be the field commander, answerable to no one but Grant, and Grant now suggested that Hunter make his own headquarters at Cumberland, or at Baltimore, or somewhere, and let the field commander operate without his direction. But Hunter had grown so discouraged by War Department interference that he told Grant he would like to be relieved altogether; that way he would be spared embarrassment, and the War Department would not have to use an officer it distrusted. Grant agreed with him, and in his memoirs noted that Hunter had shown "a patriotism that was none too common in the army" by surrendering an important command simply because someone else could fill it better.

Having attended to this, Grant wrote out a new order putting the four military departments in the Washington and Potomac area into the hands of a sort of holding company known as the Middle Military Division, and naming Sheridan as its temporary commander; then he telegraphed Sheridan, in Washington, to come to the Monocacy camp at once.

Sheridan got to the camp on August 6, and his interview with Grant was brief. Grant gave him the letter of instructions which he had written the day before for Hunter, telling him that this was to guide his conduct of operations. He explained the concentration at Halltown—by the time Sheridan arrived, hardly any troops remained on the Monocacy—and inside of two hours Sheridan was on his way to the front and Grant was heading back to City Point.

He had met and passed a crisis; that is, he had reasserted his own control of military affairs, which is exactly what Lincoln had wanted him to do.

Whether Grant and Lincoln were right or wrong in the belief that the war would be lost if a Democratic administration took control of it, they obviously did believe it, and they were quite right in arguing that the war had to be won politically as well as on the battlefield. That was what made it necessary to put up with Butler's incompetence in command at Bermuda Hundred at the same time that it was necessary to get rid of incompetence in command on the upper Potomac—and that, in the end, was why there could not be a general in high command who was genuinely nonpartisan. McClellan like Grant was a soldier who had lost his political innocence, and this fall he was accepting the fact that there was a Republican strategy and a Democratic strategy bearing profoundly different connotations. To his friend Barlow, a little after this, McClellan wrote that "Grant has gone clean over to the enemy." McClellan had his sources of information about army politics, and he saw that a good many leading soldiers were going to keep quiet until things came to a head: "Hancock is on the fence, waiting to see which is the winning side. So will many genls, including Meade. Gibbon, Hunt, Bartlett and Patrick are perfectly sound."

Frank Leslie's Illustrated Newspaper, DECEMBER 3, 1864

On Election Day Union soldiers voted in the field. At the headquarters of the Army of the Shenandoah the first two officers in line were Generals Phil Sheridan and George Crook. The soldier vote was expected to favor General McClellan; instead, most of it went to President Lincoln.

As he faced all of this, Grant was matter-of-fact, and he probably neither knew nor cared how the other generals felt about the election or about the terms on which peace could be made. Lincoln was in Washington, getting a different view of things, and at times what he saw was darkened by the haunted shadow which his own realism cast across his belief in democracy. On August 23 he wrote that strange, secret message predicting his own defeat and quietly put it away for future reference: "This morning, as for some days past, it seems exceedingly probable that this administration will not be re-elected. Then it will be my duty to so co-operate with the President-elect as to save the Union between the election and the inauguration; as he will have secured his election on such ground that he cannot possibly save it afterward."

More clearly than anyone in Washington, Grant could see that from the military point of view the war was actually going well. Since the Virginia and Georgia campaigns opened on May 4, the Confederacy had been put under the kind of continuing strain it had never before had to endure. Something was bound to give—and now, in Georgia, the collapse was beginning to take place and the soundness of Federal strategy was being emphasized by its results.

Over and over, during two months and more, Grant had told correspondents that the Confederate armies could no longer afford to make a stand-up fight in the open field. Yet near Atlanta, as July came to an end, General Hood had done just that: three times he attacked Sherman's army, trying to break its stranglehold on the city, and three times he failed; in the process he lost something like 20,000 men, many more than he could afford to lose. Steadily Sherman tightened his grip on the city and finally, on September 2, it fell. "Atlanta is ours," he wired, "and fairly won."

Grant got the news on the evening of September 4, while he was sitting in a camp chair in front of his headquarters tent, smoking a cigar and chatting with members of his staff. To the officers who were within listening distance he read aloud the telegram announcing Sherman's victory, and then he ordered Meade's and Butler's headquarters to have a 100-gun salute fired, with shotted guns, from every battery that bore on the Rebel works.

But Jubal Early was still at large in the Shenandoah Valley. After his conference with Grant on the Monacacy early in August, Sheridan had gotten off to a slow start. By mid-September Grant was growing impatient; he set off to see Sheridan face to face, "to have him attack Early or drive him out of the Valley and destroy that source of supplies for Lee's army." As it turned out, by the time Grant arrived in the valley Sheridan had a workable plan for doing just that, and Grant simply urged him to get on with it. On September 20, the day after Grant returned to his headquarters, an exultant telegram arrived from Sheridan: "I have the honor to report that I attacked the forces of General Early on the Berryville Pike at the crossing of Opequon Creek, and after a most stubborn and sanguinary engagement, which lasted from early in the morning until 5 o'clock in the evening, completely defeated him . . ."

This most violent of civil wars was about to come to its climax in the orderly formalities of a quadrennial election, because after all it was that kind of war: testing whether any nation so conceived and so dedicated could long endure. The strangest part about it was that the soldiers themselves were going to vote—those who were old enough, anyway—even though it was clear that a soldier who wanted to fight no more, disliked his generals, or had lost track of what he was fighting for would assuredly vote for the opposition, which if it won would be under strong compulsion to call the war off altogether. To give soldiers that much control over their own destiny was unprecedented, and it might well be very risky, but it was unavoidable; and now Grant had to determine how much electioneering could take place in the ranks of an army which every day in every month was engaging the enemy.

Grant took a long look at the matter, and he put his thoughts on paper in a manner showing that the head of the democracy's armies understood democracy to the full; understood that the democratic process need not be feared as long as the men who used it acted with boldness and good sense. Writing thus, Sam Grant at last came of age and turned a routine document into a triumphant affirmation of the faith America fought for. On September 27 he sent Mr. Stanton this letter:

The exercise of the right of suffrage by the officers and soldiers of armies in the field is a novel thing. It has, I believe, generally been considered dangerous to constitutional liberty and subversive of military discipline. But our circumstances are novel and exceptional. A very large proportion of legal voters of the United States are now either under arms in the field, or in hospitals, or otherwise engaged in the military service of the United States.

Most of these men are not regular soldiers in the strict sense of that term; still less are they mercenaries, who give their services to the Government simply for its pay, having little understanding of the political questions or feeling little or no interest in them. On the contrary they are American citizens, having still their homes and social and political ties binding them to the States and districts from which they come and to which they expect to return.

They have left their homes temporarily to sustain the cause of their country in the hour of its trial. In performing this sacred duty they should not be deprived of a most precious privilege. They have as much right to demand that their votes shall be counted in the choice of their rulers as those citizens who remain at home. Nay, more, for they have sacrificed more for their country.

I state these reasons in full, for the unusual thing of allowing armies in the field to vote, that I may urge on the other hand that nothing more than the fullest exercise of this right should be allowed, for anything not absolutely necessary to this exercise cannot but be dangerous to the liberties of the country. The officers and soldiers have every

On election night excited crowds waited for early returns outside the office of the New York Herald. *Four million votes were cast, and Lincoln was re-elected by 400,000.*

86

means of understanding the questions before the country. The newspapers are freely circulated, and so, I believe, are the documents prepared by both parties to set forth the merits and claims of their candidates.

Beyond this nothing whatever should be allowed. No political meetings, no harangues from soldiers or citizens, and no canvassing of camps or regiments for votes. I see not why a single individual not belonging to the armies should be admitted into their lines to deliver tickets. In my opinion the tickets should be furnished by the chief provost-marshal of each army, by them to the provost-marshal (or some other appointed officer) of each brigade or regiment, who shall on the day of election deliver tickets irrespective of party to whoever may call for them. If, however, it shall be deemed expedient to admit citizens to deliver tickets, then it should be most positively prohibited that such citizens should electioneer, harangue or canvass the regiments in any way. Their business should be, and only be, to distribute on a certain fixed day tickets to whoever may call for them.

In the case of those States whose soldiers vote by proxy, proper State authority could be given to officers belonging to regiments so voting to receive and forward votes. As it is intended that all soldiers entitled to vote shall exercise that privilege according to their own convictions of right, unmolested and unrestricted, there will be no objection to each party sending to armies, easy of access, a number of respectable gentlemen to see that these views are fully carried out.

In the end: no problem. The soldiers talked things over among themselves, soldier fashion, but there was no general electioneering to disturb army morale or discipline, and the men showed they could take a national election in their stride. As Election Day drew nearer it became quite obvious that these soldiers were not in any significant numbers going to try to vote themselves out of the war. They had affectionate admiration for McClellan, but he lost many votes in the army he once commanded because the men felt that he had been made the victim of a stop-the-war faction that had dominated the Democratic convention; men who were using great batteries of siege guns to salute immense victories were not ready to embrace a party whose platform called the war a failure. Elated Republicans in the election districts back home were boasting that they needed no campaign speeches except the dispatches from Sherman and Sheridan (although just to be on the safe side they sent out every orator they had); and the soldier vote began to look so safe that in states which had no absentee-voter laws Republican party leaders pulled wires to get the men furloughed by regiments, confident that nearly all of them would vote for Lincoln. And now, near the end of the third week in October, Sheridan sent in another dispatch which told the North that it need never again worry about Jubal Early or Confederate operations in the Shenandoah Valley. Sheridan had won another victory, and this time it was conclusive. The federal triumph at Cedar Creek virtually ended the career of Early's army.

If Grant had any doubts about how the election was going to go he kept them to himself. On election night he and his staff sat up late around the campfire in front of the Commanding General's tent, waiting for election returns, and Grant was so little worried about the outcome that he indulged in a slightly heavy-handed practical joke. According to Brigadier General M. R. Morgan, commissary general at headquarters, Grant received reports from the headquarters telegraph operator and read them out for everyone to hear; and all evening long he read telegram after telegram that showed McClellan far ahead. Most of the officers who listened to him were good Lincoln men, and some of them went off to bed dejected, convinced that Lincoln had lost. Before he himself retired, after midnight, Grant confessed (to those who had stayed up long enough to hear him) that it had all been a hoax; every report that came in, throughout the evening, had showed Lincoln in the lead.

What pleased Grant most was not merely that Lincoln had won but that this election in the middle of a civil war had gone so quietly, so much like any peacetime election, as if the country knew it was going to go on and on electing Presidents and accepting the electoral verdicts for all time to come. He expressed himself in a telegram to Secretary Stanton: "Enough now seems to be known to say who is to hold the reins of government for the next four years. Congratulate the President for me for the double victory. The election having passed off quietly, no bloodshed or riot throughout the land, is a victory worth more to the country than a battle won. Rebeldom and Europe will so construe it." He wrote to Mrs. Grant saying that he hoped the verdict of the people would be accepted everywhere: "If there was less clamor and dissention in the North the rebellion would be much sooner put down. The hopes of the South are constantly fed by the sayings of our Northern people."

Then he got down to the practical business at hand, and sent a wire to Halleck: "I suppose, without my saying anything about it, all the troops now in the North will be hurried to the field, but I wish to urge this as of the utmost importance. Sherman's movement may compel Lee to send troops from Richmond, and if he goes I want to be prepared to annoy him."

What Grant was saying was that the war was entering its final phase. General Sherman and 60,000 soldiers had left Atlanta and were beginning to march to the sea. ★ ★ ★

Two Argonnes

CONTINUED FROM PAGE 48

sector boiling, and they obeyed them with enthusiasm. Their days and nights were devoted to aggressive patrolling and limited attacks. The Germans retaliated with intense bombardments. In the history of my father's 312th Regiment, the unnamed historian tells how one of these barrages fell with special fury on my father's Company C, killing Lieutenant Donat G. O'Brien and several other men.

My father was a tough, cocky Irishman from the downtown slums of Jersey City. When the chaplain urged everyone to take the full $10,000 insurance policy the government was offering at rock-bottom rates, Sergeant Fleming had sneered: "I can take care of myself," and opted for only $3,000. After a night spent with his face in the shuddering St.-Mihiel mud with chunks of deadly metal humming around him, he signed up for the full $10,000. "I never thought I'd come out of it in one piece, after that night," he said.

At the same time, my father retained his faith in something he called "Irish luck." Those who scoffed at this superstitious philosophy must have wondered, after the death of Lieutenant O'Brien. As my father told it in later years, that first barrage caught them in the open. "You never saw anyone dig holes faster in your life," he said. "I was down about three feet when the Lieutenant crawled over to me and told me to get out, he was taking over my hole as a command post. I told him to go dig his own goddam hole. Finally he *ordered* me out, and it was go or get court-martialled." Fifteen minutes later, while Sergeant Fleming, still cursing fluently, was digging himself a new hole a few dozen yards away, a shell made a direct hit on O'Brien's command post. "All we ever found of the poor guy," my father said, "was a piece of his raincoat."

Over 2,000 Lightning men had been killed, wounded, or were missing by the time Pershing ordered the division withdrawn from St.-Mihiel for service in the Argonne. They made some of the sixty-mile journey in trucks, but most of it they covered in traditional infantry fashion, "picking up one brogan and putting the other one down," as my father liked to describe it. While they marched, they sang. The 311th Regiment's favorite was "Smile, Smile, Smile." Others preferred "K-K-K-Katy," "Mademoiselle from Armentières," or "Madelon." It was a singing war.

But this sentimental streak (on the wall of his bedroom, my father had framed the words of that saccharine song "My Buddy") was strangely combined with an almost primitive toughness. Frank Mueller, a member of Company C, told me, "The first time I saw your father, he was a bayonet instructor at Fort Dix. He made my hair stand on end, the way he'd snarl, 'Stick it into his guts and pull it out the same way!' " Going into the Argonne, Mueller recalls my father getting into an argument with one of his best friends. "We were marching along, and all of a sudden, Red just flattened him. Right there in the road. Out cold, with one punch. Nobody talked back to your old man."

Ahead were Argonne days and nights when both the sentiment and the toughness would be tested to their utmost limits.

I drove out of the Argonne Forest along a road that runs through the towns of Lançon and Senuc. My father's regiment had marched up this road on the night of October 15–16, 1918. The rain, by then a standard feature of the battle, came down in relentless sheets, and darkness was total. No one had the slightest notion where he was going. Guides who supposedly knew the way were as lost as everyone else. The confusion was par for the Argonne course. As they had moved up through the forest, the commanders of the 78th Division had been told that they would relieve the 82nd Division. They had rushed their best young officers forward, to spend days mapping and patrolling the 82nd's front. Then, without so much as a whisper of explanation, they were told to relieve the 77th, along a front about which they knew no more than they could read on their maps.

The 78th division was split into two brigades of two regiments each. Except for battalions held in reserve, both brigades were supposed to be in line at 5:30 A.M. on the morning of the sixteenth of October, to launch an all-out attack on the town of Grandpré, on the Bois de Bourgogne beyond it to the left, and on a smaller woods known as the Bois des Loges, to the right. Because of the total confusion in which they marched, both wings of the division arrived late. The second battalion of the 310th Regiment, for example, marched all night in the rain and got nowhere. At 10:30 A.M., under direct orders, they had to leave the shelter of the Argonne's trees and move across the Aire River and an open field 500 yards wide, through an enemy barrage that cost them, one veteran remembers bitterly, "more casualties than we took in two whole weeks at St.-Mihiel."

The German defenses known as the Hindenburg Line ran from the Bois de Bourgogne through Grandpré and the Bois des Loges into the little village of Champigneulle. In 1968 I sat in the farmhouse of André Godart, a bluff, barrel-chested citizen of Champigneulle who was fifteen years old when the 78th Division came across his father's fields. The Germans had tunnels running from the cellar of the family farmhouse to the forward trenches and blockhouses. Godart took me out in the pasture behind his house, and to my amazement the eye could still trace the snaking line of the German trenches, while in the distance several of the concrete blockhouses were still visible, sunk deep in the earth, with only a slit, like a baleful mouth, for machine-gun fire. Here, as everywhere in the Argonne, the deceptive contours of the rolling earth were startling. The ground fell away in a long gradual incline across naked fields all the way from Champigneulle to the Grandpré–St.-Juvin road. In 1918 those fields, Godart said, were thick with barbed wire, huge belts of it every hundred feet. In the north, the British were using 4,000 tanks to open paths through the wire for their infantry. In the Argonne, the Americans had only 189 tanks, and most of these had been knocked out the first day. All Pershing could offer his infantry were artillery barrages to blast holes in the wire. More than one soldier died trying to find holes that were not there.

I drove with Godart down the road from Champigneulle toward Grandpré. About halfway, he stopped the car and pointed across another naked field toward a clump of woods—the Bois des Loges. This was the primary objective of the right brigade of the 78th Division. It was only a few thousand square yards, but from the 78th's viewpoint it might have been designed by the devil and handed to the Germans as a gift. It was a series of ravines, like a giant corrugated iron roof, thick enough to conceal machine guns and to protect the defenders from detection by artillery, yet thin enough to give them murderous fields of fire. The men of the 309th and 310th Infantry reached the edge of the woods, but that was only Act One in a terrible two-week drama. There were machine guns every forty yards firing down the ravines. When Company F of the 310th attempted to penetrate the woods from another angle on the eighteenth of October, the Germans let them advance two hundred yards and then blasted them with machine-gun fire from both flanks. In four searing days, the 310th took 800 casualties in the Bois des Loges, and the 309th suffered proportionately.

Again and again, with unquestioning courage, the companies tried to fight their way forward, destroying one machine-gun nest only to be cut down by flanking fire from another, grappling with repeated counterattacks which, in the undemonstrative language of the 78th Division's history, "resolved" the fighting into "combats between small groups." A special feature of the nightmare in the woods was gas. The shells plopped almost soundlessly around the fighting men day and night and the deadly swirls of phosgene and mustard settled in the ravines and even in the foxholes, forcing the men to wear their uncomfortable masks almost constantly. "We slept in the damn things," one 310th man told me.

While this battle for the Bois des Loges raged, the 312th and 311th regiments were fighting their own war, in and around Grandpré. They had the same driving orders that had sent their comrades smashing into the Loges woods—attack, attack. All a visitor has to do is walk around Grandpré to realize what those words meant on October 16, 1918. A detailed exploration of the town chills the blood.

Grandpré is built against the brow of a steep hill, with a main street running east and west along the Aire River and two other streets feeding down into it from the north. The Germans controlled the north-south streets, and could infiltrate men over roofs and through back doors into the east-west houses. This was bad enough. Much worse was another German-controlled piece of local real estate which the soldiers dubbed the Citadel.

This was a tongue of rock that jutted into the center of the town and ended in a perpendicular thirty-foot cliff. Comte Bellejoyeuse, a minor figure in sixteenth-century French politics, had built his chateau on this commanding perch. The Germans had burrowed into its shattered ruins like determined moles. I climbed the hill and persuaded a lady caretaker to let me enter the grounds of the chateau, which has been restored

Although the Allies used gas against the Germans in World War I, the enemy had used it first, and doughboys in the Meuse-Argonne as elsewhere considered it a "Hun" weapon.

as a national monument. From the edge of the promontory I looked down on Grandpré and the open ground across the river beyond it, rolling out to the edge of the Argonne. From this vantage point a machine gunner could kill anyone indiscreet enough to expose himself anywhere in or around Grandpré.

This was only the beginning of the assaulters' problems. The chateau was situated in a park that stretched 700 yards behind it along the St.-Juvin road. Just beyond that was Bellejoyeuse Farm. In the division and regimental histories this ironically named farm was ranked with the Citadel and the Bois des Loges as the most agonizing obstacle in the 78th's path. The farm is still there, the same cluster of red-roofed buildings (rebuilt, of course) where the Germans had emplaced dozens of machine guns.

The day before the 78th relieved them, the 77th had filtered some men across the Aire, and in a fierce house-to-house brawl had temporarily cleared the east-west main street. Yet every man in the first patrol of the 78th that ventured into Grandpré on the sixteenth of October was killed or wounded by fire from the Citadel and the rooftops. It was obvious that an assault would have to be made in force, and the entire 312th Regiment crossed the Aire River later in the day. The rains had raised the normally rather narrow, tepid stream, and in some places the men had to wade through water up to their necks. The water ruined almost every gas mask. They had barely reached the northern bank when the Germans laid down a gas barrage. The Americans could do nothing but watch in horror as the poisonous cloud boiled up less than fifty yards away. Then what seemed to them a miracle happened. A breeze sprang up, and the deadly vapor moved down the river valley instead of enveloping them. The regiment went to work on Grandpré.

The Citadel could not be taken by frontal assault. But assailing it from the east was equally impossible. Bellejoyeuse Farm protected that flank, and the Loges woods in turn protected Bellejoyeuse Farm. The only hope seemed to be an assault that swung west of the town, up a narrow valley to a village called Talma. According to division headquarters, the French were in possession of this little town. But before the men of the 78th could move, they learned that a German counterattack had sent the French reeling back to the main road, where my father's C Company maintained an uncertain liaison with them. Machine guns were rushed to this flank, and instead of an attack, the Americans found themselves fighting a desperate defense. It was probably here that my father almost got himself court-martialled. They were dug in beside the main road, which the Germans periodically sprayed with machine-gun and shell fire. They had it zeroed in, and nothing human could live on it. To my father's astonishment, he saw a lone figure strolling casually toward them in the twilight. "Get off that road, you goddam idiot," my father roared in his best sergeant's voice. But the racket drowned him out. Another ten steps and German machine guns would cut the fool in half. With a curse my father dove out of his foxhole and went sprinting across the road to hit the stroller with a flying tackle that sent them both somersaulting off the road into a shell hole half full of rain water. An instant later the German machine guns laced the road with bullets. In the shell hole the stroller surfaced, spluttering with rage, and my father blanched to discover that he had tackled a major from division headquarters, sent out to check on the liaison with the French. The major roared about courts-martial and executions for a moment, and then looked out at the swarm of bullets tearing up the road where he had been standing a moment before. "Sergeant," he said, extending a gooey hand, "thanks for saving my life."

At Talma, as elsewhere in the Argonne, it is not so much the stories as the ground itself that makes the most eloquent history. Again and again the men of the 312th's 1st Battalion tried to push up that narrow valley, dodging, twisting, crawling from shell hole to shell hole, finally capturing a German machine-gun nest at Talma Farm, about halfway to Talma village. I walked up the valley, staring at the dark mass of the Bois de Bourgogne ahead on the left, and the steep angle of Talma Hill on the right, thinking of the morning when, their hopes raised by the capture of Talma Farm, two companies tried a surprise assault on Talma village. Shrouded by heavy fog, they moved forward and were within 300 yards of their goal when the winds of chance, which had rescued them from the gas attack, betrayed them. The fog suddenly lifted and the Germans poured in fire from the front and both flanks. Almost every man in the advance platoons was killed or wounded; the few that survived did so by playing dead through the agonizing day. At nightfall, this handful crawled back to the foot of Talma Hill.

Often men cracked in the face of such carnage. One captain, after seeing a patrol shot to pieces, asked to be relieved, claiming that his "heart" could no longer stand the strain. My father was not by nature a bitter man, but he never forgot or forgave another captain who panicked as they moved out to an assault. "I looked over my shoulder and saw him going the other way," my father said. "I would have shot the son of a bitch, but he was already intermingled with the next wave and I was afraid I'd hit one of our own men. The guys saw him later in Paris wearing a wound stripe. They walked right by him without saluting or speaking. He looked the other way."

He was less bitter about a corporal and three privates whom he had sent out one dark night to patrol the no man's land ahead of them in Talma Valley. The Germans were pouring shells into the narrow valley at regular intervals, and between barrages the smallest sound, a cough or the chink of a helmet against barbed wire, brought storms of machine-gun fire. "We had to send out these patrols because we never knew when the Dutchman might counterattack to knock us out of Talma Farm," my father said. But he admitted thinking, as the men crawled into the darkness, that it would be a miracle if they returned.

Not one came back. Sergeant Fleming returned to the grim task of keeping himself and the rest of his men alive. Five years later, he was walking down Thirty-third Street in New York. There, strolling toward him, was the corporal. Finally convinced he was not seeing a ghost, my father grabbed him and said: "I thought you were dead and buried someplace in the Bois de Bourgogne."

"Sarge," the corporal said, "I'm not stupid enough to commit suicide. When you sent us out that night, we went the other way. We didn't stop running until we were five miles behind the lines. Then we found some aid men and said we were gassed. We put on a good act and that was all there was to it."

"I bought him a drink," my father said. "What the hell. I thought about doing the same thing a couple of times up there myself."

But he kept going. So did most of the others. Why? Part of it was ethnic pride. In the Jersey City of my father's boyhood, "No Irish Need Apply" signs were common. In the Argonne, he was proving his right to be an American. So were the 78th's numerous Slovaks, Italians, Poles, and Germans.

My father loved to tell about the small, skinny Jewish private who came to him after St.-Mihiel and asked him for a transfer. He had a chance to become an assistant to the regiment's Jewish chaplain. "I don't belong in the lines with all you crazy Irishmen," the private candidly admitted. "You *like* to fight. Let me go and maybe you'll get a guy you can depend on if things get really tough." The reasoning made sense, and my father agreed to the transfer. After the war, he saw the private in Paris wearing two wound stripes. "Hymie," he said, "what the hell happened?"

"That rabbi was a madman," Hymie said. "He wouldn't stay out of the front lines. I ducked more shells than anybody in the whole damn division."

Rabbi Saul Davidowitz, the 312th's Jewish chaplain, did, in fact, win high praise in the regiment's history for repeatedly exposing himself to help the wounded under fire.

For the idealistic, the war was a genuine crusade. One Elizabeth, New Jersey, soldier, writing home a vivid description of the dead and wounded around him, added: "But all this suffering is worth it, because it will make the world safe for democracy." A few developed a savage hatred for the Germans, and killed as many as possible. Another Elizabeth man proudly told his parents of shooting Germans who had surrendered. I never heard my father, tough Mick though he was, speak a harsh word against the Germans. Once, when I was about twelve, I asked him, "Did you ever kill a German face to face?" I was surprised by how disturbed the question made him. "Maybe," he said. "I don't really remember. . . ." And he quickly changed the subject.

From their vantage points on the heights of the Bois de Bourgogne and the crest of the Talma Hill above Grandpré, the Germans were able to direct deadly artillery fire on the Lightning Division all along the line. The gun that the infantrymen hated the most was the Austrian 77 millimeter, which fired a shell they called the whiz-bang. It travelled at almost the speed of sound, so that it exploded before the man it hit even heard it. Yet by an odd twist, the German artillery helped the doughboys tolerate the Argonne's continual rain. "The muddier it got," my father told me, "the deeper the shells sank when they hit, and that cut down the shrapnel." Sixty-five per cent of the casualties, most 78th men agree, came from artillery fire. That anyone survived the rain of metal seems miraculous. André Godart told me that after the battle they counted an average of 150 shell holes to an acre on his family's farm.

On October 23, what was left of the 1st Battalion made another try at Talma. It was part of a coordinated attack that the division launched, both there and in the town of Grandpré, after a night-long artillery preparation. All the artillery accomplished was to bring down on the exhausted infantry a fierce counterbarrage that caused heavy casualties among the 3rd Battalion, fighting in Grandpré. But they went forward nevertheless, and the remnants of one squad made it to the top of the Citadel.

With the 1st Battalion, it was the same deadly story. A vicious crossfire of machine guns and artillery pinned them down on the reverse slope of Talma Hill.

They were in desperate need of artillery support, but there was no short-wave radio to get the message back to the gunners. In the A.E.F. the men in the front lines depended on runners to carry such messages. At the 78th reunion I had met a thin, wiry old man who

91

told me proudly that he had been a runner in the 311th Regiment. My first reaction had been puzzlement at his pride. Being a runner did not sound like a very glorious assignment. But he went on to tell me how one night, when the going was especially rough in Grandpré, his captain had sent eight runners back to regimental headquarters, begging for reinforcements and ammunition. All eight had been killed. He volunteered to go, and made it, crawling the last half mile with a bullet in his leg.

If that was the runner's percentage at night, his chances in broad daylight, on that terrible October twenty-third in Talma Valley, were close to zero. Yet Parker Dunn, a tough little Irish-American from Albany, New York, volunteered to risk that impossible curtain of fire. The battalion commander told him it was suicide. But Dunn, without waiting for an order, took off. He was hit once, sprang to his feet, and kept running. All around him the earth churned with shellfire and machine-gun bullets. He went down a second time. Everyone was sure he was finished. But Dunn staggered to his feet and made another few yards. A geyser of earth exploded in front of him. Dunn did not get up again. His Medal of Honor went to his stepmother.

Then came a new kind of hell. Their own artillery, groping for the range to silence the German machine guns, began falling among the prone Americans. A captain from Company D tried to reach the men who were being hit, to order them to fall back. Machine guns cut him down, and two twin brothers, Victor and Bertrand Herrmann, crawled out to help him where he lay in the open. But the captain was dead, and Bertrand Herrmann was hit. Hours later, he and the four men who tried to evacuate him on a stretcher were hit by a shell and killed instantly.

Meanwhile, members of my father's C Company somehow worked their way to the top of that shell-ripped hill and drove the Germans off it. Reinforcements from the 311th Infantry were rushed to their support. The next day, what was left of my father's company pushed into the southern edge of the Bois de Bourgogne. There, exhausted, their ranks too thin to go farther, they dug in while a battalion of the 311th Infantry drove past them.

On the night of October 27, the 312th Regiment was withdrawn and reorganized into two (instead of three) battalions. Many sergeants, including my father, were made acting lieutenants without commissions, to beef up the all but annihilated officer cadre. Around Grandpré, the rest of the 78th Division continued to extend the gains already made. Bellejoyeuse Farm was finally captured, the penetration into the Bois de Bourgogne was deepened and held

Back in the U.S.A., Americans helped keep the home fires burning with such cheerfully chauvinistic cartoons as "End of a Perfect Day," which appeared in the New York World.

against renewed German counterattacks. But the Bois des Loges remained in German hands. Ironically, my father received his only "wound" of the war coming out of the Bois de Bourgogne. The trail was blocked by a large tree branch, which each man was supposed to hold for the man behind him. Maybe a private had a grudge against the Sergeant; more probably they were all too exhausted, after nine days of almost continuous fighting, to remember the simplest order. The man ahead of my father let the branch go, and in the darkness it smashed him in the face, breaking his nose.

An officer told him to consider himself wounded and go to the rear. He refused. "I think I'm needed around here," he said. No one argued with him. The 1st Battalion had only four officers left. The regiment had lost twenty-one officers and 800 men to bullets and shellfire—and seven other officers and 150 men had been gassed and evacuated. Wiping away the blood and shrugging off the pain, Sergeant Fleming stayed with his men.

That night, back in the forest near Senuc, they found that the rear area of the Argonne was almost as dangerous as the front lines. German long-range guns, perhaps alerted by an aerial observer who had spotted a careless light or a fire, poured a terrible bombardment into the 312th's camp. That surprise attack was one of the few painful memories of the Argonne that my father shared with me. They dove under wagons and into ditches while the big shells screamed in, one after another, like berserk express trains. Suddenly one of his closest friends cried out, "Teddy, I'm hit. I'm hit." My father crawled over to him through the shellfire and asked him where he was hurt. "My legs," he said. "My legs." My father groped for his legs in the darkness, but there was nothing there. Minutes later the man was dead. My father never told me his friend's name, but the sorrow in his voice made me understand for the first time why the song "My Buddy" meant so much to him.

I prowled into the Bois de Bourgogne and the Bois des Loges. I walked around Talma and Talma Farm. I stared down the forbidding slope from Bellejoyeuse Farm toward the Aire River and the bare fields beyond it. Every foot of the ground was amazingly unchanged from the descriptions in the regimental and divisional histories. A blink of the eye, a flick of a time-machine switch, and these same fields and woods were torn by shellfire and littered with the bodies of my father's friends once more.

In the Bois de Bourgogne, André Godart's hunter's eyes spotted a rusted, grisly relic of the battle, a German helmet. He gave it to me as a souvenir. Standing in silence on Talma Hill, the helmet in my hands, I struggled to assess what I was learning. There was a gulf between this experience and the old soldiers' reunion stories, the tales told by my father and his friends. They did not begin to approach the reality that these tan, naked fields and shrouded woods evoked. More significant, the tellers had not really tried. Most of the time they only hinted at what they had seen and heard. Suddenly I was remembering my father's refusal to talk about killing Germans, and I was hearing a sentence someone spoke at the 78th's reunion: "Five minutes in combat made a man out of anybody—if he came out of it standing up."

Now I know what you have left out, I thought. The horror. But I also understood, far more deeply, the pride. Pride that required no boasting, no verbiage, not even testimony. For those who had been through the Argonne, it was enough to say: "I was there."

The men of the 78th had accomplished the dirty job assigned to them. The task recalls the harsh larger reality of the Argonne as described by Laurence Stallings, author of *The Doughboys*: "No one, corps or army commander, expected the 78th to capture the German positions before them. Their assignment was to exert flank pressure by exposing themselves in a series of attacks to contain an enemy seeking to sideslip toward the center where . . . the 42nd and 32nd Divisions were ripping into his heart."

Pershing's strategy, a war correspondent said, "called for violent pressure on his [the enemy's] flanks in order to draw forces from his center." Thus the grim historical truth about the sacrifices of my father and his friends. Thus the explanation for the frantic insistence on repeated attacks, often without artillery, from their very first day in the lines.

In the over-all American sector, during those ten days of bitter flank fighting, Pershing completely reorganized his forces from the top down, creating two separate armies to guarantee better communication between headquarters and the front. More artillery was moved up and fresh or rested divisions came into the line. On November 1 the offensive resumed with a mighty roar, and the hammer stroke was delivered at the German center.

Up over Barricourt Heights went the doughboys, smashing a huge hole that made a retreat on the flanks inevitable. For one more day the Germans punished the 78th in the Bois des Loges and the Bois de Bourgogne, but the next morning (November 2) the men of the 310th pushed ahead and found only a few dead Germans left behind by their departed comrades. Sometimes using trucks, but going most of the way on foot, the 78th galloped twelve miles in exhausting pursuit of the fleeing enemy. At Boult aux Bois my father's C Company joined hands with a French detachment in a tumultuous celebration. The union of the two armies in this town, just north of the Bois de Bourgogne, meant that the end was near.

But the German soldier was still a deadly foe. On November 5, a patrol of the 309th Infantry entered the village of Sy. The French civilians assured them the Germans were still very much on the run. About a kilometer beyond the town, machine guns spat from surrounding ridges. One officer managed to fight his way out. Every other man in the patrol was killed, wounded, or captured. It was a bitter postscript to the division's twelve-mile advance and, to compound the irony, it was the 78th's last day in battle. That night, the 42nd Division replaced them and the Lightning Division marched out of the Argonne. My father had preceded them. He and several other sergeants were pulled out on November 3 and sent to officers' training school.

This last small item of personal history illuminates John J. Pershing's iron resolve to ignore rumors of imminent peace that had filled American newspapers throughout October and November. Even when he was finally told (on November 1) that Berlin was seeking an armistice, Pershing drove his men forward with the same attack-and-the-hell-with-your-flanks order. He quite agreed with Marshal Foch that the German army had to be defeated in the field, if the spectre of Prussian militarism was to be stamped out forever. But the politicians decided that they could not afford to risk Pershing's policy of unconditional surrender. So with doughboys looking down on Sedan from the heights of the Meuse, and with allied artillery shelling the jugular Metz–Lille railway, the roaring furnace of the Argonne fell silent on November 11, 1918. In the front lines, men looked at each other in amazement, unable to believe that they were going to survive after all. Like my father, every doughboy who spent a day under fire had long since resigned himself to the inevitability of his own death.

The last place I visited in the Argonne was the American Cemetery on the heights above the town of Romagne. Fourteen thousand of the Argonne's 44,000 dead sleep here. It is still the largest American overseas cemetery. Row on row the white marble crosses stretch across the beautifully sculptured grass. Above them on a small rise is a chapel with stained-glass windows carrying the insignia of each American division, the 78th's lightning patch among them. I looked, and thought about battles and history.

Could I re-create the reality of the Argonne? As history, yes. I could see it with a clearer, colder eye. I could give reasons, make analyses that my father and his friends, struggling through the shell-churned mud, simply could not consider. But as for recapturing those singing, brawling doughboys, what they really thought and felt about the rain-soaked, shell-shrieking days and nights, with the constant smell of death in the mind and in the nostrils, no. Their garrulous reticence (for that, I finally decided, was the only way to describe it) may be explained by a line Guy Chapman records in his story of the British front in World War I, *A Passionate Prodigality*. "The war, old chap, is our youth, secret and interred." But I suspect a larger explanation. The Argonne was the last enormous expression of *America*'s youth and perhaps they sensed the tragedy, sensed that this marvelous innocence had been violated there by old Europe's grimmer, more terrible vision of life and death. Never again, after the Argonne, would we go to war with a smile and a song.

Time has created two Argonnes. Mine, a thing of words and terrain and memory, belongs to my generation. My father's sleeps with him and his friends beneath the crosses at Romagne and other cemeteries, or hides beneath the banter at division reunions. Both are true.

Mr. Fleming, a regular contributor, went to France under AMERICAN HERITAGE *auspices to gather material for this article. He wishes particularly to thank Edgar H. Barber, superintendent of the American Cemetery at Romagne, for help in arranging visits to the Meuse-Argonne battlefields. Recommended further reading: Laurence Stallings'* The Doughboys *(Harper & Row, 1963).*

The Memorable Assassination

And who is the miracle-worker who has furnished to the world this spectacle? All the ironies are compacted in the answer. He is at the bottom of the human ladder, as the accepted estimates of degree and value go: a soiled and patched young loafer, without gifts, without talents, without education, without morals, without character, without any born charm or any acquired one that wins or beguiles or attracts; without a single grace of mind or heart or hand that any tramp or prostitute could envy him; . . . an inefficient lackey; in a word, a mangy, offensive, empty, unwashed, vulgar, gross, mephitic, timid, sneaking, human polecat. And it was within the privileges and powers of this sarcasm upon the human race to reach up—up—up—and strike from its far summit in the social skies the world's accepted ideal of Glory and Might and Splendor and Sacredness! It realizes to us what sorry shows and shadows we are. Without our clothes and our pedestals we are poor things and much of a size; our dignities are not real, our pomps are shams. At our best and stateliest we are not suns, as we pretended, and teach, and believe, but only candles; and any bummer can blow us out. . . .

It was a swift celebrity the assassin achieved. And it is marked by some curious contrasts. At noon last Saturday there was no one in the world who would have considered acquaintanceship with him a thing worth claiming or mentioning; no one would have been vain of such an acquaintanceship; the humblest honest boot-black would not have valued the fact that he had met him or seen him at some time or other; he was sunk in abysmal obscurity, he was away beneath the notice of the bottom grades of officialdom. Three hours later he was the one subject of conversation in the world, the gilded generals and admirals and governors were discussing him, all the kings and queens and emperors had put aside their other interests to talk about him. And wherever there was a man, at the summit of the world or the bottom of it, who by chance had at some time or other come across that creature, he remembered it with a secret satisfaction, and *mentioned* it—for it was a distinction, now! It brings human dignity pretty low, and for a moment the thing is not quite realizable—but it is perfectly true.

The remarks above were written in September, 1898, after the Empress Elizabeth of Austria was stabbed by an alleged anarchist on a street in Geneva. As it happened, the Empress was of slight political importance, and her violent death has been nearly lost in the shadows of history; but Mark Twain's reflections on the incident have, unhappily, an apparently timeless relevance. The excerpt is reprinted from the book What Is Man?, *a collection of essays by Mark Twain; copyright 1917 by the Mark Twain Company, copyright renewed 1945 by Clara Clemens Samoussoud; reprinted by permission of Harper & Row, Publishers.*

A Reasonable Doubt

CONTINUED FROM PAGE 43

Decatur she stuck to a plain, unembroidered story, as lacking in specific details as possible. She and Leibowitz often shouted back and forth at each other, but whenever the attorney uncovered contradictions in her testimony, she would retreat into vagueness: "I can't remember," or "I ain't sure, that has been two years ago."

"When you got to the doctor's office, were you not crying in any way?" Leibowitz asked. "I had just hushed crying, the best I remember I was crying—I won't say, I ain't positive," Victoria said crossly. To the attentive courtroom, Leibowitz recalled Mrs. Price's story in the original trials: that she and Ruby had gone to Chattanooga looking for work and on the night of March 24 had stayed at Mrs. Callie Brochie's boardinghouse on Seventh Street. The next morning, both girls had testified, they fruitlessly searched for a job in the city's cotton mills before boarding the Huntsville-bound freight at 11 A.M.

Leibowitz pointed out that Mrs. Price had said Mrs. Brochie's house was three or four blocks from the train yards. Wouldn't you rather say it was two miles? asked Leibowitz. "No sir, I wouldn't say two miles," she replied. "Suppose I told you that Seventh Street in Chattanooga, the nearest point . . . to the railroad yards of the Southern Railroad is two miles and show you the map, would that refresh your recollection?" he asked sarcastically. "I don't know," retorted an equally sarcastic Victoria, "I haven't got a good enough education." When he challenged her entire account of the overnight stay in Chattanooga, she broke in, shouting, "That's some of Ruby Bates's dope," and added: "I do know one thing, those Negroes and this Haywood Patterson raped me." Leibowitz stood and stared at her for a moment. She was, he told her, "a little bit of an actress." "You're a pretty good actor yourself," she quickly replied.

After a few questions about her activities on the day before the alleged incident, the tone of Leibowitz's voice suddenly changed. Gravely, he asked Mrs. Price: "Do you know a man by the name of Lester Carter?" She thought he was one of the white boys thrown from the train, she replied. "Mrs. Price, I . . . want to ask you that question again and give you an opportunity to change your answer if you want to," said Leibowitz. "Did you know Lester Carter before that day, Yes or No?" By his intense expression, spectators in the courtroom knew the question was crucial; they leaned forward to hear her answer. Mrs. Price, losing her composure for the first time, mumbled: "Before in Scottsboro—he—was on the train." "I didn't ask you that," said Leibowitz. "Before this day on the train did you know Lester Carter?" "I never did know him," she said firmly.

He continued in the same low voice. Had she asked a companion of hers "to pose as your brother, since you didn't want the authorities to know you were travelling across the state line from Chattanooga . . . [with] somebody with you?" Mrs. Price looked to the table where Knight sat and then back at Leibowitz. "If I said that I must have been out of my mind." "Did you say it?" he asked firmly. Shouting, she clenched the arms of her chair. "If I said it I must have been out of my mind!"

Leibowitz questioned Mrs. Price about Jack Tiller, the married man with whom she had been convicted of adultery. "Did you have intercourse with Tiller a short time before you left Huntsville [for Chattanooga]?" She shook her head emphatically. "In the railroad yards?" he asked, still in the same quiet voice. "I have told you three times, and I am not telling you any more—no, sir, I didn't." Leibowitz returned to Carter. He asked her again if she had arranged with Carter, or "whatever man that was with you, [that] he wasn't supposed to know you on the train because you were afraid to cross the state line and [were afraid of] being locked up for the Mann Act?" She turned angrily to Judge Horton: "I haven't heard no such stuff," she shouted. "That is some of Ruby's dope he has got."

Relentlessly the chief defense attorney continued to probe. He asked Mrs. Price once more where she had spent the night before the alleged assault. Perhaps in a hobo jungle? he asked slyly. Victoria stared at him, her eyes filled with hatred. Columnist Mary Heaton Vorse, one of only two women in the courtroom, found it impossible to describe her "appalling hardness." Only two years before, reporters had described Mrs. Price as "pretty and vivacious." Now, with her hair tightly curled in a new permanent and her face heavily rouged, she seemed more than "tough," Miss Vorse wrote. She was "terrifying in her depravity." Through clenched teeth Mrs. Price repeated again the account of how she had stayed with Mrs. Brochie while she looked for work. Leibowitz asked her if she didn't want to change her story. She shook her head. "By the way, Mrs. Price," said Leibowitz with open disgust, "as a matter of fact, the name of Mrs. Callie [Brochie] you apply to this boardinghouse lady is the name of a boardinghouse lady used by Octavius Roy Cohn in the *Saturday Evening Post* stories—Sis Callie, isn't that where you got the name?" Knight jumped to his feet in protest and Judge Horton sustained his objection. Leibowitz, however, had dramatically made his point;

he was pleased with the results of his cross-examination.

The prosecution, concerned about the damaging effects of Leibowitz's questions, re-examined Mrs. Price in order to impress upon the jurors the gravity of the charge. Without the "flutter of an eyelash and in a voice that carried to the furthest corner of the courtroom" (wrote one reporter), she related in the most specific Anglo-Saxon terms the sexual demands made upon her by the defendants. Leibowitz knew the only purpose of the re-examination was to inflame the emotions of the jurors. In a voice shaking with anger he sarcastically asked Mrs. Price: "You are not embarrassed before this huge crowd when you utter these words?" "We object," exclaimed Knight, while Mrs. Price looked at Leibowitz with such venom that one reporter thought she was going to strike him. Suspecting that Victoria's fear of the Mann Act had led her to accuse the Negroes, Leibowitz explained that he had only one more question. "I want to ask you if you have ever heard of any single white woman ever being locked up in jail when she is the complaining witness against Negroes in the history of the State of Alabama?" Without waiting for her answer or Knight's objection, Leibowitz angrily took his seat at the defense table.

> **GIRL REPEATS STORY IN SCOTTSBORO CASE**
>
> State's Witness at Decatur Trial Screams Denial of 'Framing' Negro Defendants.
>
> **MORAL ATTACK RULED OUT**
>
> Judge Rejects Court Records as Not Affecting the Credibility of Her Testimony.
>
> *New York Times, APRIL 4, 1933*

The last witness for the state on Monday was Dr. R. R. Bridges, one of the doctors who had examined the girls shortly after the alleged rape. Bridges' testimony and that of his younger colleague, Dr. M. W. Lynch, had been crucial for the state's case at Scottsboro. Under cross-examination, however, Leibowitz brought out facts that made the doctor a stronger witness for the defense than for the state. Bridges admitted that less than two hours after the alleged rape both girls were completely composed and calm, with normal pulse and respiration rates, and no pupil dilation. Even though Mrs. Price claimed she had been brutally raped six times, the doctor testified that there was no vaginal bleeding and that he and Dr. Lynch had had great difficulty finding enough semen to make a smear slide. The semen they did find was completely nonmotile. Bridges readily admitted that this was unusual: spermatozoa normally live from twelve hours to two days in the vagina.

The following morning, Attorney General Knight explained to Judge Horton that the state did not intend to call Dr. Lynch, since his testimony would be repetitious. After Horton's consent, however, a bailiff whispered to the judge that the young doctor urgently wanted to speak to him—in private. The only room available in the crowded building was one of the courthouse restrooms, and there the two men talked. Lynch, visibly unnerved, went straight to the point. Contrary to Knight's explanation, said Lynch, his testimony would not be a repetition of Dr. Bridges', because Lynch did not believe the girls had been raped. From the very beginning, said the Scottsboro physician, he was convinced the girls were lying. Even Dr. Bridges had noted at the examination that the vaginal areas of the two women were "not even red." "My God, Doctor, is this whole thing a horrible mistake?" asked the stunned Horton. "Judge, I looked at both the women and told them they were lying, that they knew they had not been raped," replied the doctor, "and they just laughed at me."*

Horton sent for Knight and confronted him with Lynch's statement. Knight was adamant. It was only the opinion of one doctor, he insisted, and the state was committed to the prosecution of the nine boys.

Judge Horton, now doubting that any rape had occurred, faced a painful dilemma. He could force Dr. Lynch to take the stand or he could himself, by Alabama statute, end the trial. In either case, Lynch—because of his courageous act—would be ruined. In his mind, Horton went over the twelve jurors who sat on his left. He knew more than half of them personally and—in spite of their conventional southern attitude toward Negroes—he believed that the weight of the evidence presented by the defense would convince them of Patterson's innocence. With many misgivings, he decided to allow the trial to continue.

Before the state rested its case on Tuesday afternoon, Knight called to the stand five additional witnesses. Their testimony was inconclusive, and it became clear that the case would stand or fall on the testimony of Victoria Price.

In planning his defense, Leibowitz realized that normal legal assumptions could not be made at this trial. Usually a defense lawyer has only to prove that there is reasonable doubt of his client's guilt. In Decatur, Leibowitz knew he would have to prove beyond a reasonable doubt that Patterson was innocent.

His first witness was Dallas Ramsey, a Negro who

---

* This account, based upon recent interviews and correspondence with former Judge Horton—and carefully checked by him in manuscript form—has been emphatically denied by Dr. Lynch, who wrote to the author on October 16, 1967, that as "far as I can recall, no such statements were ever made to Judge James E. Horton or anyone else regarding the trial of Haywood Patterson versus Alabama. Of course, it has been 35 years and better since this incident happened; and as far as I can recall, I was never put on the stand as a witness in this case."

lived near the hobo jungle in Chattanooga. He testified he had seen and talked with two white girls and two white men on the evening of March 24 and the morning of March 25, 1931. Ramsey picked Mrs. Price from the courtroom as one of the women; from a photograph he identified Ruby Bates. The four had apparently stayed the night in the wooded vagrant's refuge near his home.

George W. Chamlee, a prominent white Chattanooga attorney, took the stand next. He told the jury he had made dozens of personal inquiries and examined city directories in an effort to locate Mrs. Price's "boardinghouse friend," Callie Brochie. He was convinced, he said, that Mrs. Brochie was a figment of Victoria's imagination. No woman by that name had lived in Chattanooga between 1930 and 1933.

Then Leibowitz took a calculated risk. One by one he put six of the Scottsboro boys on the stand. The jury, he knew, would surely discount their insistence that they were innocent; and, if they made an unfavorable impression, Patterson's conviction would be assured. But Leibowitz had to dispel the state's image of the youths as malevolent conspirators acting coldly and methodically to throw the white boys from the train and then rape the two defenseless white girls.

The first two boys who testified were tragic representatives of a society's deprivation and neglect. Homeless, unemployed, illiterate, they had wandered across the South since their early teens. Willie Roberson, short and stocky and with a wild shock of hair, sat quietly in the courtroom with a vacuous stare. Syphilitic since birth, he spoke with a severe speech impediment. At the time of his arrest, he was in great pain from open venereal sores, and walked with a cane. (Four years later a psychiatric examination disclosed a mental age of nine and an intelligence quotient of sixty-four.) Olen Montgomery was blind in his left eye; with his right he could see "good enough not to get hurt, that is all." Yet Victoria Price had identified them "positively" as two of the defendants who had run across the top of a moving boxcar, leaped into the gondola where she sat, fought a pitched battle with the white boys, and then brutally raped her. Montgomery and Roberson told the courtroom they had been riding back toward the rear of the train and had not even known of the disturbance until they were arrested at Paint Rock.

On the witness stand Ozie Powell, Eugene Williams, Andrew Wright, and Haywood Patterson readily admitted participating in the fight. Williams and Patterson, who were travelling with the two Wright brothers (Andy and his twelve-year-old brother, Leroy), explained that somewhere between Chattanooga and Stevenson several whites had begun throwing rocks at them and shouting, "Black son-of-a-bitches." Patterson said that he had rounded up the other Negroes who were hitching on the train to "have it out." Most of the white youths leaped from the gondola before actually being hit. After the fight, the victorious blacks scattered across the train. Unanimously the Scottsboro boys insisted they had not even seen, let alone molested, the two white girls. Patterson in particular, tall, black, and ostentatiously unservile, held his own during Knight's stormy questioning. When the Attorney General made some reference to Patterson's having been tried at Scottsboro, he was bluntly corrected. "I was framed at Scottsboro," declared the young Negro. Knight, flushed with anger, demanded, "Who told you to say you were framed?" Patterson retorted: "I told myself to say it."

It is doubtful whether the testimony of the Scottsboro boys had any effect, one way or the other, on the deliberations of the jurors, for it was Leibowitz's scathing cross-examination of Mrs. Price that preoccupied Alabamians. Anyone "possessed of that old Southern chivalry," said the Sylacauga *News*, could not read of the "brutal" harassment of Mrs. Price without "reaching for his gun while his blood boils to the nth degree." Within hours after Victoria stepped from the witness stand, reporters overheard angry threats on the streets of Decatur. On Wednesday, Judge Horton learned that a "mass indignation rally" had been held the night before in the local Masonic hall. Several of the two hundred men at the meeting bluntly demanded that the "New York Jew lawyers" be tarred, feathered, and ridden out of Decatur on a rail. For the Scottsboro boys, the prescription was summary justice from the nearest tree.

A grim-faced Judge Horton ordered the jury removed from the courtroom, and then, in a voice betraying deep emotion, he told the spectators that the guilt or innocence of Haywood Patterson and his fellows was for the jury alone to decide. He wanted to make it absolutely clear, he said, that the court intended to protect the prisoners and their attorneys. "I say this much, that the man who would engage in anything that would cause the death of any of these prisoners is a murderer; he is not only a murderer, but a cowardly murderer." For the first time in the trial Horton raised his voice. Anyone who attempted to take the lives of the prisoners "may expect that his own life be forfeited," he sternly told the silent courtroom. "I believe I am as gentle as any man . . . I don't believe I would harm anyone wrongfully." But he added, emphasizing every word, that there would be no compromise with mob violence. "Now, gentlemen, I have spoken . . . harsh words, but every word I say is true and I hope we will have no more of any such conduct. Let the jury return."

Horton's stern warning ended the open threats of violence. But according to reporters, it also seemed to intensify the community's bitter hostility.

Now under round-the-clock protection by National Guardsmen, Leibowitz continued doggedly to hammer away at the state's case. To intensify the impact for the defense of Dr. Bridges' testimony, he called to the stand Edward A. Reisman, a Chattanooga gynecologist who had spent all his life in Alabama and Tennessee. After reviewing all the medical evidence, Dr. Reisman declared that in his professional opinion it was "inconceivable" that Mrs. Price had been raped six times, as she claimed. But the spectators completely distrusted Dr. Reisman. As one Decatur resident told the *New York Times* reporter, "When a nigger has expert witnesses, we have a right to ask who is paying for them." On Thursday morning Leibowitz presented his most damaging witness. Lester Carter, a twenty-three-year-old hobo, had been on the train when the fight began; it was his name that had so startled Mrs. Price during Leibowitz's cross-examination. Now, wearing a new gabardine suit and a brightly flowered tie, Carter added graphic details to the story Leibowitz had previously sketched. In January of 1931, Carter testified, a Huntsville police court had convicted him of vagrancy and sentenced him to sixty days in the county workhouse. There he met Victoria Price and her boyfriend, Jack Tiller, who were serving time for adultery. When the three were released in March, Tiller invited Carter to stay around Huntsville for a few days. The hospitable Mrs. Price even offered to arrange a date for Carter with her best girl friend, Ruby Bates. On the night of March 23, approximately forty hours before the alleged rape, Tiller and Carter met the two girls outside the gates of a local mill. Talking and giggling, they walked to the Huntsville hobo jungles.

"What occurred in the jungles that night?" asked Leibowitz. "I hung my hat on a little limb and went to having intercourse with the girl [Ruby]," replied Carter. Less than three feet away, Tiller and Victoria also were "having intercourse." When a light rain began to fall, the four got up from the honeysuckle bushes where they had been lying and crawled into an empty boxcar pulled onto a sidetrack. During the night, in the intervals between love-making, they "talked and started planning this hobo trip," he said. The girls complained that they were sick of Huntsville; perhaps they could go to Chattanooga and "hustle" while the two men got temporary jobs. Tiller explained that he did not want to risk another adultery conviction, but he promised vaguely to meet the other three in Chattanooga if they did not return in a few days. Just before daybreak, the girls went home and collected a change of clothes. They agreed to meet Carter in the freight yards that afternoon.

On the way to Chattanooga, Carter explained, he pretended he did not know the girls; they rejoined each other only after leaving the train. Just beyond the railroad yards, they met Orville Gilley, a slender, self-styled "hobo poet." After Gilley introduced himself, they walked together to Chattanooga's hobo jungle, built a small fire, and shared a meager meal of chili and coffee. During the night, Carter told the court, he once again had sexual relations with Ruby Bates. He could not say for certain about Victoria and their new friend.

The next morning, the four decided they had seen enough of Chattanooga. Tired and hungry, they boarded the 11 A.M. freight for Huntsville. Five white hobos sat in the next car toward the caboose. Just south of Stevenson, Alabama, Carter said, he heard several shouts above the noise of the train. He investigated and saw white and Negro boys fighting in the adjoining car. By the time he and Gilley could get there, however, most of the white youths had jumped or been shoved from the train. Without striking a single blow, Carter "climbed down where the couplings are" and got off. Gilley remained behind. In Scottsboro several hours later, Gilley denied there had been any rape, said Carter.

Although Carter testified persuasively and was unshakable in cross-examination, the jury and spectators listened with open skepticism. His eagerness to testify, his frequent nervous gestures, and his immaculate appearance, one observer said, gave the impression that the defense had "carefully schooled" him. Carter's most damaging mannerism was his insistence on saying "Negro," instead of the typical white southern pronunciation, "Nigra." In cross-examination, Morgan County Solicitor Wade Wright, who was assisting Knight, drew from Carter an admission that the defense had paid his room and board for almost a month and had even bought him the "fancy" new eleven-dollar suit he was wearing.

Shortly after noon on Thursday, the defense rested

New York Times, April 7, 1933

GIRL RECANTS STORY OF NEGROES' ATTACK

Ruby Bates Makes Dramatic Reappearance at Alabama Trial to Deny Assault.

SENT BACK BY DR. FOSDICK

Girl Came to New York for Work and He Advised Her to 'Tell the Truth.'

SHE ACCUSES MRS. PRICE

Declares the Latter Concocted Her Testimony to Avoid Arrest on a Moral Charge.

"with reservations," but Leibowitz had scarcely taken his seat when a messenger brought a note to his table. Walking over to the bench, Leibowitz whispered to Judge Horton, who then announced a brief recess. The courtroom remained quiet but visibly excited. Ten minutes later, National Guardsmen opened the back doors of the room. A heavy-set, perspiring woman in her forties came down the aisle; Ruby Bates walked behind, her eyes fixed on the floor. The spectators leaned forward with an audible gasp; at the prosecution table there was open consternation. Miss Bates's chaperone, a social worker from the Church of the Advent in Birmingham, explained that the church rector had asked her to bring the young woman to Decatur. The chaperone knew nothing about the case.

Ruby was dressed in a smart gray coat with matching cloche. In 1931 an investigator for the American Civil Liberties Union had described her as a "large, fresh, good-looking girl" with soft "calflike" eyes. But the freshness now was gone. Unlike the spirited Victoria, Ruby seldom raised her eyes from the floor as she mumbled her testimony. Leibowitz asked few questions in his direct examination. On the night of March 23, 1931, "did you have intercourse with Lester Carter . . . ?" "I certainly did," Ruby replied softly. "Did Victoria Price have intercourse with Jack Tiller . . . in your presence?" he asked. "She certainly did," said Ruby. Judge Horton, who had been sitting behind the bench throughout the trial, got up and moved down to a seat in front of the spectators facing Miss Bates.

Did any rape take place on the Chattanooga-to-Huntsville freight train? continued Leibowitz. Not that she knew of, Ruby replied, and she had been with Victoria Price for the entire trip. While the jury and spectators strained to hear her low voice, she explained why she had decided to testify for the defense. Five weeks before, she said, she had left Huntsville with a boyfriend to avoid any involvement in the new Decatur trials. First she had gone to Montgomery; from there she had hitched a ride to New York, where she had worked for a "Jewish lady" for several weeks. But her conscience bothered her, and after reading about a famous New York minister, Dr. Harry Emerson Fosdick ("Dr. Fostick," she called him), she visited him in his study one evening late in March. He arranged for her to go to the Birmingham Church of the Advent and from there to Decatur. Leibowitz completed his questioning in less than fifteen minutes.

For a moment, the Attorney General stared silently at Ruby, who sat with her eyes downcast. "Where did you get that coat?" he finally asked. She hesitated for a moment, and then whispered, "I bought it." "Who gave you the money to buy it?" Knight asked. "Well, I don't know," she replied evasively, her eyes still fixed on the floor. "You don't know?" Knight repeated sarcastically. "Where did you get that hat? Who was the beneficent donor?" There was a long pause as Ruby sat biting nervously at her lower lip. From his seat inside the spectators' rail, Judge Horton leaned forward and gently asked her, "Do you know?" Almost inaudibly she murmured, "Dr. Fostick of New York."

Whenever Knight questioned her about her testimony at Scottsboro, she repeated over and over: "I told it just like Victoria Price told it," or "I said it, but Victoria told me to." The majority of the Attorney General's questions were not, however, about her earlier allegations at Scottsboro. He seemed more intent on proving to the jury that Ruby had been bribed by the defense. Knight suspected that her conscience had been given an assist by representatives of the International Labor Defense. Firing his questions rapidly at the subdued witness, he asked her about her finances. How much money was she making when she left Huntsville? How had she paid for the trip from Montgomery to New York? Who gave her funds for the trip back to Alabama? Although she talked vaguely of loans from her employer in New York, her obvious lack of candor brought smirks and open laughter from the packed courtroom. The Attorney General also drew from Ruby an admission that she was suffering from syphilis and gonorrhea in May of 1931 and had told a Huntsville doctor who treated her that she had contracted it from Negroes who had raped her.

The main testimony in the trial ended when Ruby Bates meekly stepped from the witness stand late Thursday afternoon. Her story caused "an immediate and bitter reaction among the residents of . . . [Morgan] and neighboring counties," said the *New York Times* correspondent. Citizens of the area were convinced she had "sold out" to the defense. Although Attorney General Knight expressed confidence that the "mob spirit" would exhaust itself in harmless talk, reporters noticed that Miss Bates was hustled away from the courtroom and taken to a secret hiding place by a detachment of National Guardsmen. Knight also strengthened the National Guard unit guarding Leibowitz and Brodsky.

On the following afternoon County Solicitor Wright began the state's summation. Renowned among local all-day singers, Wright bellowed his remarks in the singsong chant of a sawdust-trail evangelist. At first he rambled on about the "fancy New York clothes" of the defense's chief witnesses, Lester Carter and Ruby Bates. But soon he was ringing the changes on all the fears and hatreds that had been aroused in the two weeks of the trial. In summarizing the testimony of Carter, he said with mincing sarcasm: "What does Mr. Carter tell you, maybe it is Carterinsky now! If he had a-been with Brodsky another two weeks he would have been down here with a pack on his back a-trying to sell you goods. Are you going to countenance that sort of thing?" From a front-row seat, an excited spectator exclaimed "No!" with the fervor of an "Amen" in church.

As Wright's anti-Semitic tirade poured out, Leibowitz sat at the defense table with a look of stunned disbelief. Attorney General Knight stared fixedly at the floor, his face flushed with embarrassment. The faces of several jurors betrayed their excitement. Horton sharply reprimanded the solicitor, but Wright went tumbling on, almost lost in his own rhetorical fervor. He turned and pointed a finger at the counsel table where Leibowitz and Brodsky sat. "Show them," he paused for effect, "show them that Alabama justice cannot be bought and sold with Jew money from New York." Leibowitz leaped to his feet, slamming his hand on the defense table. "I move for a mistrial," he said. "I submit a conviction in this case won't be worth a pinch of snuff in view of what this man just said." Horton scolded Wright for his "improper statements" but refused to end the trial.

> **NEGRO FOUND GUILTY IN SCOTTSBORO CASE; JURY OUT 22 HOURS**
>
> Verdict Carries Sentence of Death After One Juror Had Held Out for Life Term.
>
> **DEFENSE SCORES FINDING**
>
> Leibowitz Terms It a Mockery of Justice While Lauding Fairness of Judge.
>
> *New York Times, April 10, 1933*

Leibowitz, facing the unenviable task of restoring calm to the feverish courtroom, began his closing remarks late in the afternoon. "Let us assume the prosecution is prejudiced," he began. "Let us assume the defense is also prejudiced. Let us assume both sides are trying to prove their points." He looked squarely into the face of each juror. "It is the sworn duty of each of you," he told them, to convict only upon "hard evidence," not emotion. He summarized the four days of testimony and emphasized what several state officials were admitting privately: that the prosecution's case rested solely on the testimony of Victoria Price. And her story, he said, was the "foul, contemptible, outrageous lie . . . [of] an abandoned, brazen woman."

The defense attorney continued his summation the next morning. By ten o'clock his voice had begun to crack with fatigue. Several times he took a few sips of water, pausing as if to gather his strength. He recalled Wade Wright's tirade, referring to it as a "hangman's speech." "What is it but an appeal to prejudice, to sectionalism, to bigotry?" Wright, he maintained, was simply saying: "Come on, boys! We can lick this Jew from New York!" The jury's verdict, he concluded, would show whether Alabamians would give even this "poor scrap of colored humanity" a "fair, square deal."

When the weary Leibowitz took his seat, Attorney General Knight began the final arguments for the state. In an obvious reference to Wright's tirade, he shouted: "I do not want a verdict based on racial prejudice or a religious creed. I want a verdict on the merits of this case." Knight exhorted the jurors to stand up for Alabama; he expressed his confidence that they were not "cowards." Referring scornfully to the almost forgotten Patterson as "that thing," he told the jury in a tone of unveiled contempt: "If you acquit this Negro, put a garland of roses around his neck, give him a supper, and send him to New York City." There, he said, "Dr. Harry Fosdick [will] dress him up in a high hat and morning coat, gray-striped trousers, and spats." Only one verdict was possible: death in the electric chair.

Horton delivered his charge to the jury before noon. He began with a pointed reference to the state's star witness, Victoria Price. The law was designed to protect all classes of people, he said, but the law also had a "stern duty to perform when women of the underworld come before it." It was the obligation of the jury, in evaluating Mrs. Price's testimony, to weigh her background of promiscuity and prostitution. In an effort to calm the emotionally charged courtroom, the judge concluded with a plea for the jury to put aside extraneous matters. "We are not trying lawyers," he said. "We are not trying state lines. We are not trying whether the defendant is black or white." The only duty of the jury was to ascertain whether there was a reasonable doubt about the guilt of Haywood Patterson. If there was a reasonable doubt, he emphasized, then they should return a verdict of not guilty. Horton, visibly exhausted from the wearing two-week trial, gave the case to the jury just before one o'clock.

The courtroom was soon empty except for lawyers and newspapermen. Patterson and the other Scottsboro boys sat in their cells and played cards or sang gospel songs to pass the time. When the jury still had not reached a decision at 11:30 P.M., Horton ordered them locked up for the night, and told them to resume their deliberations the following morning, Sunday, at 8:30 A.M.

They reached a verdict at 10 A.M. Leibowitz and Brodsky hurried over to the courthouse. There they found Patterson—guarded by two militiamen—sprawled in a chair and smoking a cigarette. Across the room, Knight sat at the prosecution table, the muscles of his face twitching nervously. When Judge

Horton arrived at 11 A.M., he called for the jury; the court stenographer opened his notebook to take down the last words of the trial. As the jurors filed in they were still laughing from a joke; they became solemn when they saw the tense courtroom.

"Have you agreed upon a verdict?" Horton asked the foreman. He replied, "We have, your honor," and handed a heavily creased slip of paper to the bailiff, who laid it on the judge's bench. Horton unfolded the slip of paper and read the large pencilled letters: "We find the defendant guilty as charged and fix the punishment at death in the electric chair." There was not a sound in the courtroom as spectators craned to see the defense table. That night a shaking Haywood Patterson would clutch a prison Bible in fear, but he had decided beforehand he would never show his inner terror to the gawking white spectators. His face did not change expression. Leibowitz looked as though he had been struck; he leaned back slackly in his chair.

After the jury had been dismissed and a postponement of further trials announced, Leibowitz walked to the bench and grasped Horton's hand. The judge warmly returned the handshake. "I am taking back to New York with me a picture of one of the finest jurists I have ever met," said Leibowitz, his voice shaking with emotion. "I am sorry I cannot say as much for the jury which has decided this case against the evidence."

Later, reporters learned from several jurors that they had not even discussed, much less considered, the testimony of Ruby Bates. The twelve men had taken their first ballot five minutes after the judge gave them the case. The vote was: guilty 12, not guilty 0. The rest of their deliberation time had been taken up with the question of the sentence. Eleven jurors had voted immediately to send Patterson to the electric chair. One, the foreman, had held out until Sunday morning for life imprisonment.

On June 22, 1933, ignoring a warning that he was jeopardizing his own chances for re-election, Judge Horton granted a defense motion and overturned Haywood Patterson's conviction. In a devastating indictment of the state's case, he concluded that Victoria Price's testimony was not only uncorroborated, but also improbable and contradicted by evidence which "greatly preponderates in favor of the defendant." To reporters, Horton implied he would also reverse any future convictions based upon her testimony.

Defense attorneys hoped that Horton's meticulous and persuasively written decision would cause a shift in public opinion in the state. It did not. At the instigation of Attorney General Knight, Horton was removed from the case and another jurist more amenable to the state's position was appointed. (The warning to Judge Horton was not just a threat: in the 1934 Democratic primary he lost his seat on the bench, despite a vigorous campaign. That same year, Attorney General Knight was elected lieutenant governor.) When Patterson and Clarence Norris, another of the Scottsboro boys, were tried again in December of 1933, both received the death sentence. In 1934, the United States Supreme Court accepted the defense contention that Negroes were systematically excluded from Alabama's juries and gave Patterson and Norris another trial. But in 1936, Patterson was convicted for the fourth time and received a sentence of seventy-five years.

The following year, the state began prosecution of the remaining eight defendants, and in rapid succession juries convicted Clarence Norris, Charley Weems, Andrew Wright, and Ozie Powell. But Lieutenant Governor Knight was dead by this time, and the state was in a mood to compromise. Instead of death, the assistant attorney general had asked only for life imprisonment. In the midst of the trials, it was suddenly announced that the state would dismiss the charges against the remaining four defendants. Although Willie Roberson and Olen Montgomery had already spent six years in jail, it was admitted that they were "unquestionably innocent." Since Leroy Wright and Eugene Williams had been only twelve and thirteen years of age in 1931, "the State thinks that the ends of justice would be met ... by releasing these two juveniles on condition that they leave the State never to return." On this grotesque note, the public story of Scottsboro came to an end.

Of the five who remained in jail, Patterson successfully escaped to Detroit years later, and eventually died of cancer in a Michigan jail. The other four were finally paroled. Andrew Wright, the last of the parolees, left prison nineteen years after he had been taken from the freight train in Paint Rock.

In 1939, Victoria Price offered to recant—for a substantial fee. No one cared to pay it. She and Ruby Bates both died in the same year, 1961, in towns thirty miles apart.

The book from which this article is adapted started as a doctoral thesis; it will be published under the title Scottsboro: A Tragedy of the American South *by the Louisiana State University Press in January, 1969. The twenty-eight-year-old author, Dan T. Carter, is an assistant professor of history at the University of Maryland. We are proud to introduce this exciting historian in* AMERICAN HERITAGE.

Dearest Friends

CONTINUED FROM PAGE 13

had repealed the Stamp Act! Yet even this he knew was but a temporary reprieve. The "Sons of Liberty" were brawling in Boston's cobbled streets; inevitably, gunfire suddenly crackled between a mob and British regulars.

The well-advertised "massacre" was somewhat different from Paul Revere's inflammatory engraving. On a bitter March night in 1770, a mob had taunted a group of regulars, some of them also hurling chunks of ice and wood. Tempers and musketry exploded, and five Americans died. Captain Thomas Preston and seven enlisted men were jailed.

The next morning one Crown lawyer after another refused to take their case. But not John Adams: his self-righteousness and his instinct for martyrdom, as well as for justice, stood by him. (See "The Boston Massacre" in the December, 1966, AMERICAN HERITAGE.) His estimation that this was "as important a case as was ever tried in any court or country of the world" may have been an exaggeration, but every man was due a fair trial. Witnesses lied. Mobs pelted Adams with mud balls, crashed rocks through his windows. He stood firm. "Facts are stubborn things," he told the court; they could not be altered.

Preston was acquitted; there was no proof that he had given any order to fire. Two of the "lobster-backs" were found guilty of manslaughter and were branded; the others went free. The law, said John Adams, "is deaf, deaf as an adder, to the clamors of the populace."

Grudgingly, Boston conceded not only his talents but his courage. Shortly afterward he ran for the legislature, or General Court, winning 418 votes out of 536. His fellow townsmen chose him moderator of a mass protest meeting at Faneuil Hall. Then the thunderbolt exploded. John Adams was named to represent Boston and the Commonwealth of Massachusetts at the Continental Congress in Philadelphia.

He set out with high hopes. He had never left New England before, and he was looking forward to good company, good conversation, and to seeing something of the world. But as John moved onto a broader stage, Abigail retreated to a narrower one. She was back in Braintree on the bleak farm of her bridal days. Boston Harbor was bottled up; civil war threatened.

John's letters from Philadelphia were necessarily and disappointingly "Tittle Tatle." He was sworn to secrecy on the doings of the Continental Congress. Even so, he had urged Abigail to put his letters "up safe." (She did.) "They may exhibit to our Posterity," he wrote, "a kind of Picture of the Manners, Opinions and Principles of these Times of Perplexity, Danger and Distress." News from home was more immediate —and disturbing. Drought was parching New England, and even his "poor Cows," Abigail wrote in jest, addressed him a petition for his consideration.

He was home for Christmas and a few intense, close-packed weeks before galloping to Philadelphia again. Their separation would be for months this time. Both knew the storm was gathering. Never would Abigail feel more fervently the need of "a Friend who shares our misfortunes and afflictions." The past October she had celebrated her tenth wedding anniversary—alone. She knew now that the pattern of her marriage was fixed—for years, perhaps; she would be alone weeks and months at a time. The children's crises, their education, the household tragedies—all were hers to bear alone. Nor could he share the responsibility by mail. At the very least a letter took ten to twelve days in transit, sometimes as long as three weeks.

Abigail heard the thunder. Only it was not thunder; it was a fine clear June day in 1775. Suddenly she knew. With eight-year-old John Quincy, she rushed to the summit of nearby Penn's Hill, which commanded a clear view of Boston Harbor and the slopes of Breed's Hill and Bunker Hill beyond. Huge coils of black smoke were swirling over Charlestown, and rowboats filled with crouching men were moving out across the harbor between Boston and Charlestown.

"Powder and artillery," shouted John in Philadelphia, "are the most efficacious . . . conciliatory measures we can adopt." Now, upon his motion, Congress voted to raise a Continental army and to name a commander in chief. John approached the man they had in mind, and a week later in Braintree Abigail looked up into the blue eyes of a very tall and travel-wearied man, described by her husband as "the modest and virtuous, the amiable, generous and brave George Washington Esqr."

This was the one bright moment in a summer of incredible hardship. Since April, refugees had been pouring out of besieged Boston and into Braintree, filling every room of every house. Food had to be provided, meals cooked, bed linen and clothing washed, and comfort supplied. The Adams house was inundated; the children's rooms became virtual dormitories.

By late summer, an inevitable dysentery epidemic swept the area. Abigail nursed her husband's brother Elihu, who lay in racking agony until he died. Next, a serving man fell ill; then Abigail herself, lightly; then the youngest boy, Tommy; then two young serving girls, Susy and Patty. Almost hourly the coffins moved to the churchyard; some families lost three, four, or five children. Patty lay dying for five weeks, "the most shocking object my eyes ever beheld," Abigail confessed. The little girl, who had been a member of the household for four years, literally wasted away and would let no one but Abigail near her. Simultaneously, Abigail had to nurse her mother. She buried them both within ten October days, sustained mainly by her faith and the survival of her children.

Abigail was living from letter to letter during those hard days. A lapse of some weeks after Washington's visit brought an outburst: "I want some sentimental Effusions of the Heart"; then her aching heart was eased when five letters arrived all at once. "My best Friend," John told her, ". . . all the Friendship I have for others is far unequal to that which warms my heart for you." He only wished that he could write "more than once" every day, but he was still bound to secrecy and working eighteen hours a day.

John's Christmas homecoming was muted this year. So many familiar faces were gone. His usually somber cast of mind was burdened with the sorrow of knowing that the break with Britain was nearing at last. In January Washington raised the flag of "the United Colonies" or "the Grand Union." But the war itself went badly. The British fleet still prowled the coast. The Army camps were rife with disease. Grimly, John surveyed a potter's field, a "Congregation of the dead." The smallpox, he knew, took ten of Washington's men for every one that perished by the sword.

In Braintree the night quiet of March 2, 1776, was mutilated with cannonading. Footsteps sounded; the men of Braintree were marching out. All night the firing continued, rocking the house. Two nights later, in a nocturnal maneuver that astonished the British, Washington moved 3,000 well-equipped men to the heights of Dorchester above Boston. Then came incredible news: the British were pulling out.

With peace restored to Boston, nine-year-old Johnny became a post rider between the city and Braintree; smiling slyly, he would hand his mother first one and then another and another of the hoped-for letters. Now she and the children were in more danger from the smallpox than from the British. "Will you come and have the small Pox here?" John wrote suddenly to Abigail. "Let me please myself with the Thought." Abigail would not; she had made a drastic decision. Smallpox was still ravaging the army. Terrified men were having themselves secretly inoculated, then were passing the disease on in its hideous "natural" form through the exchange of paper currency, which eventually got back to the civilians. Abigail would take no further chances. On July 12 she and the children slipped secretly into Boston, taking with them a cow, a load of hay, some bedding, an old nurse, and a nursemaid who had had "the distempre." Once arrived, they moved into a Beacon Hill mansion fronting a fruit orchard, lent to them by John Hancock. And there Abigail had herself and all the children inoculated.

Abigail's mother considered her daughter's fiancé socially inferior, even though her own home hardly compared with the Adams' homestead, above, in Braintree (now Quincy), where John was born in 1735.

John heard the news from others before her July 13 explanation arrived. "I suspect, that you intended to have run slyly, through the small Pox with the family, without letting me know it," he protested, "and then have sent me an Account that you were all well. This might be a kind Intention, and if the design had succeeded, would have made me very joyous. But the secret is out, and I am left to conjecture." He longed to be with his family. But he could not leave. After the heady achievement of the Declaration of Independence, Congress had bogged down in a significant discussion over the proposed Articles of Confederation: the question was whether each colony should vote as one, or in proportion to its numbers.

"I hang upon Tenterhooks," John wrote on July 27. "Fifteen days since, you were all inoculated, and I have not yet learned how you have fared. But I will suppose you all better and out of Danger. Why should I torture myself when I cant relieve you?"

Abigail came through her own brief but severe siege only to find that her plan for an incarceration of only a month or so was a vain hope. For the children, all inoculated at the same time, were taking the disease successively or not at all, thus leaving the laggards open to infection "in the natural way." Frenziedly, she had them inoculated again and again; the process was seemingly no longer the simple matter that it had been during John's mild session twelve years before.

Wearily, she longed for the campaign to be over. By late August, Nabby was studded at last with "6 or 7 hundred boils," each the size of a pea; she could not stand or sit. A few days later the doctor said that she was doing well, but "tis hard to make her think so." Charles was inoculated three times, then sank into a stupor. He had taken smallpox "in the natural way."

The children's convalescence dragged on. August was all but over. Abigail found a quiet spot and sat down with her pen:

Boston August 29 1776

Dearest Friend

I have spent the 3 days past almost intirely with you. The weather has been stormy, I have had little company, and I have amused my self in my closet reading over the Letters I have received from you since I have been here.

I have possession of my Aunts chamber in which you know is a very conveniant pretty closet with a window which looks into her flower Garden. In this closet are a number of Book Shelves, which are but poorly furnished, however I have a pretty little desk or cabinet here where I write all my Letters and keep my papers unmollested by any one. I do not covet my Neighbours Goods, but I should like to be the owner of such conveniances. I always had a fancy for a closet with a window which I could more peculiarly call my own.

Here I say I have amused myself in reading and thinking of my absent Friend, sometimes with a mixture of paine, sometimes with pleasure, sometimes anticipating a joyfull and happy meeting, whilst my Heart would bound and palpitate with the pleasing Idea, and with the purest affection I have held you to my Bosom till my whole Soul has dissolved in Tenderness and my pen fallen from my Hand.

How often do I reflect with pleasure that I hold in possession a Heart Eaqually warm with my own, and full as Susceptable of the Tenderest impressions, and Who even now whilst he is reading here, feels all I discribe.

Forgive this Revere, this Delusion, and since I am debared real, suffer me, to enjoy, and indulge In Ideal pleasures—and tell me they are not inconsistant with the stern virtue of a senator and a Patriot.

I must leave my pen to recover myself and write in an other strain. I feel anxious for a post day, and am full as solicitious for two Letters a week and as uneasy if I do not get them, as I used to be when I got but one in a month or 5 weeks. Thus do I presume upon indulgance, and this is Humane Nature, and brings to my mind a sentiment of one of your correspondents viz. "That Man is the only animal who is hungery with His Belly full." . . .

I am sorry to find from your last as well as from some others of your Letters that you feel so dissatisfied with the office [chief justice of the superior court of Massachusetts] to which you are chosen. Tho in your acceptance of it, I know you was actuated by the purest motives, and I know of no person here so well qualified to discharge the important Duties of it, Yet I will not urge you to it. In accepting of it you must be excluded from all other employments. There never will be a Salery addequate to the importance of the office or to support you and your family from penury. If you possess a fortune I would urge you to it, in spight of all the flears and gibes of minds who themselves are incapable of acting a distintrested part, and have no conception that others can.

I have never heard any Speaches about it, nor did I know that such insinuations had been Thrown out.

Pure and disintrested Virtue must ever be its own reward. Mankind are too selfish and too depraved to discover the pure Gold from the baser mettle.

I wish for peace and tranquility. All my desires and all my ambition is to be Esteemed and Loved by my Partner, to join with him in the Education and instruction of our Little ones, to set under our own vines in Peace, Liberty and Safety.

Adieu my Dearest Friend, soon, soon return to your most affectionate   Portia

Four days later she awoke to "a Beautifull Morning. I see it with joy, and I hope thankfullness. I came here with all my treasure of children, have passed thro one of the most terible Diseases to which humane Nature is subject, and not one of us is wanting." How much more beautiful it would be if John were home. She had reason now to believe that Congress would soon complete its business. New delays arose. "I have been here, untill I am stupified. If I set down to write even to you, I am at a Loss what to write," John reported on the seventh of October. When he could not write, he confessed, he felt more pain than did Abigail when she waited and heard nothing, but he simply did not have time. On October 11, he abruptly announced: ". . . I am coming to make my Apology in Person."

Two months and nine days they shared together. Then John rode off into the northern January cold of 1777 to return to Philadelphia. "When I reflect," he wrote en route from Baltimore, "upon the Prospect before me of so long an Absence from all that I hold dear in this World, I mean all that contributes to my private personal Happiness, it makes me melancholly. When I think on your *Circumstances* I am more so, and yet I rejoice at them in spight of all this Melancholly.—God almightys Providence protect and bless you and yours and mine." Abigail was pregnant.

Never had John Adams so longed to be at home. He sent tender messages and letters to the children, reminding young John that "a Taste for Literature and a Turn for Business, united in the same Person, never fails to make a great Man. A Taste for Literature, includes the Love of Science and the fine Arts. A turn for Business, comprehends Industry and Application as well as a faculty of conversing with Men. . . ."

Now it was John's turn to wait anxiously for letters. Abigail was weary, but her health was only one of her pressing concerns. There was no molasses, no mutton, no pork or lamb. There was no sugar, no coffee, no tea. There was almost no flour. In Boston the bakers doled out a loaf of bread a day to large families, and in June women raided a city storehouse for flour. "A Dollor now is not eaquel to what one Quarter was two years ago. . . ." Abigail thereupon resolved to buy no more clothes, even if the family became like Eve and Adam; nor would she pay black-market prices for

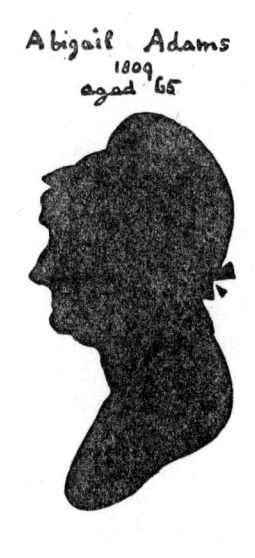

In 1809, John and Abigail, still very much "Dearest Friends," sat for these silhouettes by Charles Willson Peale's son Raphael. The inscriptions were written by their son, John Quincy.
COLLECTION OF DAVID M. FREUDENTHAL

meat. She paid with her health instead. She felt well enough, but was pale as "a whited wall." John Quincy told her: "Mar, I never saw any body grow so fat as you do." By June she was really ill, and, as if sensing her condition, her husband was looking forward to mid-July with more anxiety than he could describe. "You will have Patience with me," he begged, for this time away would be the last. Now he was going to "bid farewell to great Affairs. I have a Right to spend the Remainder of my days in small ones." But the loss of her company and "that of my dear Babes for so long a Time, I consider as a Loss of so much solid Happiness."

It was now July. Abigail could not sleep. Two weeks more to wait for the baby. Six months more to wait for John's return. "Do you sigh for Home?" she had written. "And would you willingly share with me what I have to pass through?"

His "answer" crossed her query in transit:

Philadelphia July 10. 1777. Thursday
My Mind is again Anxious, and my Heart in Pain for my dearest Friend. . . .

Three Times have I felt the most distressing Sympathy with my Partner, without being able to afford her any Kind of Solace, or Assistance.

When the Family was sick of the Dissentery, and so many of our Friends died of it.

When you all had the small Pox.

And now I think I feel as anxious as ever.—Oh that I could be near, to say a few kind Words, or shew a few Kind Looks, or do a few kind Actions. Oh that I could take from my dearest, a share of her Distress, or relieve her of the whole.

Before this shall rea[c]h you I hope you will be happy in the Embraces of a Daughter, as fair, and good, and wise, and virtuous as the Mother, or if it is a son I hope it will still resemble the Mother in Person, Mind and Heart.

It was as if he had sensed the tragedy. For a week Abigail had been severely ill. On the night of July 8 she was taken with "a shaking fit," which left her almost certain "that a life was lost." The next evening she received a letter from John to "My dearest Friend."

Those three words meant more to her than any other part of the letter except the close of it. "I wanted the personal and tender soothings of my dearest Friend, that [ren]derd it so valuable to me at this time." The next day she went into labor, and it was her fears, not John's hopes, that were realized. Both had had their hearts set on another daughter. But the "fine looking" little girl never opened her eyes. Twelve-year-old Nabby cried for hours.

John received Abigail's and the doctor's letters about the twenty-eighth of July. Never in his life had he been so moved, and devoutly he gave thanks to God for sparing the one dearest to him in all the world. Yet he sorrowed bitterly for the lost baby. "Is it not unaccountable, that one should feel so strong an Affection for an Infant, that one has never seen, nor shall see? Yet I must confess to you, the Loss of this sweet little Girl, has most tenderly and sensibly affected me."

Abigail's health and spirits bounded back with their customary elasticity. She looked forward eagerly to her husband's homecoming; the sight of his clothes in the closet "raise[d] a mixture both of pleasure and pain in my Bosome." But she found comfort in the blooming of the farm. "Heaven has blessed us with fine crops," she wrote. There was more hay than last year and two hundred bushels of corn. They would have "fat Beaf and pork enough," and enough cloth for homespun to clothe the servants and children. There would be "butter and cheese enough." The fruit was poor, but there was plenty of garden "sause" (vegetables).

In Philadelphia, John was reaping a different kind of harvest. The tide of war had finally begun to turn for the colonial cause. Recruits were swelling the depleted ranks, and although the approach of Sir William Howe had forced Congress to flee Philadelphia, John was optimistic about the final outcome. There was militia enough—if it would stand and not run away. The people were calling for blood; Washington was "getting into the Humour of fighting." At Germantown, as at Brandywine, the Continentals had withdrawn in an orderly manner after a brief, abortive attack. But for a few moments they had fought like veterans. Then came wonderful news, "a Capitulation of Burgoine and his whole Army." Shortly afterward, John could write: "Howe is compleatly in our Power."

Three years had elapsed since John Adams had "stepped into the Coach . . . to go to Philadelphia in Quest of Adventures." Adventures he had had, in plenty. But he had had enough. He was going home, going back to Abigail, who after thumbing through "a feast of Letters" had ended a recent letter: "Good Night Friend of my Heart, companion of my youth —Husband and Lover—Angles watch thy Repose."

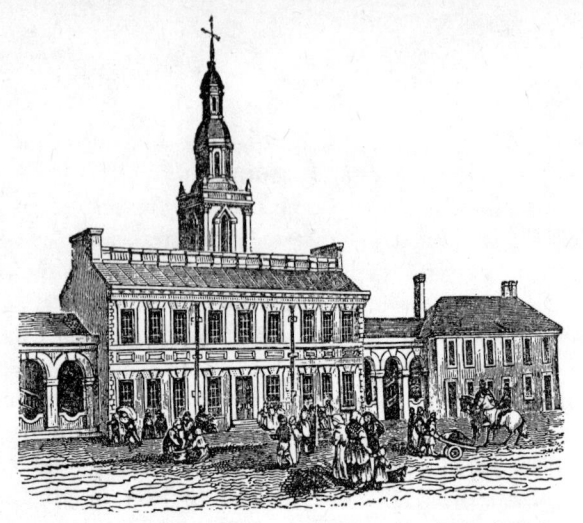

John spent most of his three-year service with the Continental Congress in Philadelphia's State House, where the Declaration of Independence was signed and which is now known, of course, as Independence Hall.

Delay after delay halted his return. Not until November 14, 1777, could he write from Easton, Pennsylvania: "Here I am.—I am bound home.—I suppose it will take me 14 days, perhaps 18 or 20, to reach Home."

For John and Abigail, now, it was as if the guns were stilled, the peace won and complete. Abigail had a husband again; the children, a father; the cup of happiness for them all was brimming over. John's absences now were the old, familiar ones, riding the law circuit and back again in a few days' time.

It was during one of these periods that, according to John's instructions, Abigail opened an ominous and official-looking document—and sank into cold despair. She read it over and over, her heart chilling. John Adams had been named a commissioner to France.

Had he not sacrificed enough? Had not she? Passionately—in letters to James Lovell, who had written John urging him to accept the appointment, and to her friend Mercy Warren—she railed out against this "plot against him," this scheme to rob her of all her earthly happiness. Her husband had been home for only a few weeks. His children needed "the joint force of his example and precepts." Should she now "consent to be seperated from him whom my Heart esteems above all earthly things, and for an unlimited time"?

In her anguish she resolved to let John decide for himself, although she feared what his answer might be. They had already spent over half of their married life apart. Welling up in them both were all the "tender sentiments that years have encreased and matured." When John was "in the Dumps," which was frequently, he could write that he went "mourning in my Heart, all the Day long . . . for myself a Frock and Trowsers, an Hoe and Spade, would do for my Remaining Days." But then there were moments when his friends called him "the Zeal-Pot," when he gloried in his heart and head and hands and what he could do with them for his fellow men, and gloried too that the partner of all his joys and sorrows shared in his struggle to build their young country.

Abigail bowed her head. She knew what she must do. John must finish his work. She would throw no impediment in his way. John felt little hesitation. Although he, no less than Abigail, knew the cruelty of separation, his sense of duty, coupled to his ambition, resolved the dilemma for him. Letters urging him to accept were pouring in upon him. And he knew the truth of what Lovell had written him, that the Continental Congress must have "a man of inflexible Integrity on that Embassy."

Later, perhaps, Abigail and the children might join him. But not now, not with British men-of-war prowling the Atlantic. The little twenty-four-gun frigate *Boston* might be sunk and all of them lost. But he would take one child, ten-year-old John Quincy. The boy needed his father; furthermore, he was old enough to profit from foreign travel.

Abigail tried to stifle her sorrows by work, by outfitting her men for the bitter six weeks' winter crossing. Shirts must be made, and there was no cambric to be had. Ample supplies of tea, chocolate, apples, and cider must be packed aboard, and ink contrived from gunpowder for the longed-for letters. Would she ever hear from her dear ones? she wondered; there might be sea battles, storms. But she steeled herself, silenced all complaints. "None knew the struggle it has cost me," she confessed afterward. Few human beings had "so valuable a treasure to resign." She could not bear to go to Boston to watch that tiny ship move out into the gray bleakness of the Atlantic. She parted from young John and her "Best of Friends" at home, in the familiar surroundings where they had said farewell so many times before.

"Great necessities call out great virtues," she wrote John Quincy afterward. Hers was sacrifice. She could not read the future. She could not know that she would later join her husband abroad, that she would shine at the French court, that she would become her country's first Vice President's lady and the second First Lady. Now she could only sit down at her desk, take out her pen, and once again write the words, "Dearest Friend."

Miss Coit, the author of six books, won a Pulitzer prize in 1951 for her biography John C. Calhoun: American Portrait. *The quotations from the letters of John and Abigail Adams are reprinted by permission of the publishers from* Adams Family Correspondence, I and II, *L. H. Butterfield, Editor; The Belknap Press of Harvard University Press. Copyright 1963 by The Massachusetts Historical Society.*

The Awkward Interval

CONTINUED FROM PAGE 7

terms beginning March 4 in odd-numbered years, dating from when the government was organized under the Constitution. Consequently, although members of the House were elected in November of even-numbered years, their predecessors' terms did not expire until the subsequent March 3. Unless there was a special session, a newly elected member would not take his seat for thirteen months—until December of the year following his election. His first or "long session" ran from December of the odd-numbered year until summer of the even-numbered year. That fall there would be a new election. After the election the member, whether re-elected or not, would return for the "short session" until March; if he had been defeated at the polls, he was a "lame duck." (The term seems to have originally been used in the eighteenth century to denote a stock market speculator who got caught short; by the time of the Civil War it had migrated to the lexicon of politics.)

In the early years of the Republic there may have been sufficient reason why congressmen elected in November could not take their seats a month later. Men of substance were not accustomed to setting off on short notice for stays of several months' duration, and, as we have seen, three weeks or longer might have been required just for the travel from some of the southern or western states. But as transportation improved, the spectacle of defeated or retiring politicians sitting in Congress while men with fresh mandates remained at home seemed increasingly anomalous. In addition to being politically obsolescent, the Congresses of the short sessions often displayed behavior that ranged from irresponsibility to venality, as representatives who had been retired by their constituents sought to salvage something financial or political from the wreckage, or at least to enjoy a last fling in Washington.

"Lame duck" thus acquired an increasingly disdainful connotation. Each time there was a change in the White House the country was governed for four months by a superseded President and—in part at least—by a lame-duck Congress. It was an awkward time at best. Presidents retiring after the customary limit of two terms, or even those who were retiring voluntarily after one, usually managed to survive the interval with reasonable dignity, although they found that there was little they could do, or that anybody wanted them to do, except say farewell. A President who sought re-election and failed, however, was not only lame but (to borrow the Biblical expression) halt. Having been repudiated, he found his influence almost nil; and even if he managed to get a few things done, alone or in conjunction with Congress, neither the country nor the new President was likely to thank him. Presidential lame ducks may not have been as irresponsible as their congressional counterparts, but they have been even more pathetic.

The first President to be turned out of office by the voters was John Adams. Although deeply wounded in spirit, he grimly plowed ahead with unfinished business during his last weeks. Congress, dominated by other lame-duck Federalists, co-operated. Adams arranged and the Senate ratified a diplomatic convention that settled a number of outstanding problems with France. But Adams also used his appointive powers in a way that aroused partisan controversy. John Marshall, a Federalist tower, was made Chief Justice. On Adams' recommendation, Congress expanded the federal judiciary, creating twenty-three new judgeships in which Federalists were promptly installed. Minor executive and judicial appointments took care of a number of other Federalists, including both a nephew and a son-in-law of the President. As late as March 2, Adams nominated forty-three justices of the peace for the District of Columbia; they were confirmed on the third. That evening, Adams signed the commissions for these appointees and left town without waiting for his successor's inauguration. Although Federalists maintained that in making these appointments Adams was merely doing his duty, the "midnight judges" were viewed quite differently by Republicans, many of whom expressed indignation.

Ironically, the second President rejected for re-election by the voters was the son of the first. John Quincy Adams started his Presidency under a cloud of controversy over an alleged "corrupt bargain" with Henry Clay that had put him in the White House—the offer of a job as Secretary of State in return for Clay's support. After experiencing heavy political weather for four years, Adams was beaten decisively by Jackson in 1828. Perhaps recalling his father's experience, he avoided further serious controversy between November and March; his administration, as the historian James Schouler put it, "preserved a dignified composure before the country." The President proposed little and Congress did little except to bestow, in favored states, liberal subsidies for canals and other internal improvements. Congress declined to confirm most of Adams' appointments, and the outgoing President was keenly disappointed at its failure to approve one of his pet projects, a proposed exploring expedition to the South Seas. President-elect Jackson arrived in Washington the day Congress counted the electoral vote, but, embittered by political attacks on his late wife, he declined to call on the President, and Adams declined to make the first move. Thus another party turnover occurred without amenities between old and new Presidents; like his father, Adams did not attend the inauguration of his successor.

Perhaps the longest tenure in lame-duck status was that of Andrew Johnson, who fought with Congress during most of his time in the White House and was left virtually powerless for almost a year after his narrow escape from conviction following his impeachment in the spring of 1868. The Republican party, dominated by the Radicals, rushed to nominate General Grant, and although Johnson nursed hopes for the Democratic nomination, his own party considered him untouchable. After the election, tensions seemed to be relaxed and Johnson enjoyed a considerable amount of personal if not political good will. Apparently with nothing else to do, he presided over several splendid social events at the White House that winter; he had many visitors, and even some of those who had led the impeachment came around to shake his hand. Five thousand people turned up at Johnson's last reception, two days before the end. President-elect Grant, though, was not welcome, and Johnson avoided the inauguration.

At best, however, presidential turnovers during the Gilded Age were accompanied by an undignified amount of scrambling for office and preferment both in Congress and the executive. "This is the moment," said Henry Adams in *Democracy*, "when the two whited sepulchres at either end of the Avenue reek with the thick atmosphere of bargain and sale."

Another accidental President who spent almost four years in limbo was Chester A. Arthur, who succeeded after the assassination of Garfield in 1881. A former New York machine politician whose rise to the Presidency dismayed many, Arthur surprised both friends and enemies by the uprightness of his administration. He made some excellent appointments, urged tariff reform, and vetoed pork-barrel bills—which were passed over his veto. After Democratic victories in the 1882 congressional elections, there was an interesting demonstration of what a lame-duck Congress could do: in recognition of demands for reform, and not incidentally to protect some Republican appointees against the Democratic storm that was coming, Congress passed the Pendleton Act, which laid the foundation for the civil service merit system. By 1884 Arthur was a half-success—which of course was fatal, and he was passed over for renomination.

To Grover Cleveland belongs the unique distinction of having been a presidential lame duck twice. Renominated but defeated for re-election in 1888, he managed to exit with reasonable grace as Benjamin Harrison occupied the White House. Four years later Cleveland was back, but his second term proved less successful than his first: he was buffeted by an economic panic, fights over the tariff, the Pullman strike, and the greenback issue. During the last two years of his term he found himself wedged between a Republican Congress and his own party, which was increasingly drawn to what Cleveland considered soft-money heresies. The final break with the Democrats came in 1896, when Bryan was nominated and Cleveland supported the Gold Democrat splinter group. Now politically isolated, Cleveland spent his final months freely exercising the veto power and striving unsuccessfully to cool the excitement over Cuba that eventually led to war with Spain.

Speaking literally, the biggest lame duck was the amply constructed William Howard Taft, whose renomination in 1912 split the Republican party and left Taft to run last in a three-way race, behind both Woodrow Wilson and Theodore Roosevelt. Taft's conduct after his defeat contributed largely to his historical reputation for geniality. Before leaving the White House he made several good-tempered speeches, participated in an active social season, puttered with schemes for government reorganization and a budget system, and took an ocean voyage to inspect the Panama Canal. Congress had already gone Democratic in the mid-term elections and was content to mark time waiting for Wilson. The legislators ignored most of Taft's modest recommendations, killed some of his administrative reforms, passed pork-barrel bills, and declined to confirm some 1,400 postmasters and other nominees to make sure that there would be plenty of jobs open for deserving Democrats.

Although by present standards it was still a simple government with simple problems, by the end of Taft's term there was beginning to be concern about the waste of time in the old-fashioned system of presidential and congressional replacement. Taft also was dissatisfied with the prevailing custom that restricted communication between outgoing and incoming Presidents, especially if they were of different parties, to polite notes and conversation on inauguration eve concerning housekeeping in the executive mansion. Without fully revealing his purposes, Taft made several inquiries through intermediaries, and finally wrote to Wilson directly to invite him to confer at the White House in December, 1912. But Wilson, who had just taken a month's vacation in Bermuda, now claimed to be too busy.

Shortly before Wilson's inauguration an event occurred that demonstrated the dangers of both the leisurely transition schedule and the limited communication between outgoing and incoming administrations. In February, 1913, violent revolution broke out in Mexico; American lives were endangered, and there was clamor for U.S. intervention. Taft tried to wait it out and avoid commitments that his successor would have to live with, but the situation was volatile and he was not certain this stand could be maintained. On February 25, Secretary of War Henry Stimson publicly suggested that members of the future Wilson Cabinet come forward for conversations about the Mexican situation. However, Wilson refused to take the Mexican business seriously and was not ready to reveal his Cabinet selections; in fact, at that moment he had not even picked a Secretary of War.

Four years later, having tasted presidential responsibility and being deep in diplomatic maneuvers on the eve of World War I, Wilson grew concerned about the interregnum that would occur if he failed of re-election against Charles Evans Hughes in November, 1916. He put the lame-duck problem succinctly in a note to his Secretary of State:

Four months would lapse before he [Hughes] could take charge of the affairs of the government, and during those four months I would be without such moral backing from the nation as would be necessary to steady and control our relations with other governments. I would be known to be the rejected, not the accredited, spokesman of the country; and yet the accredited spokesman would be without legal authority to speak for the nation. The direction of the foreign policy of the government would in effect have been taken out of my hands and yet its new definition would be impossible until March.

Wilson's proposed solution to the problem reflected his study of British institutions. In order to turn over the government promptly to the people's choice, he would appoint the President-elect as Secretary of State, and then both he and his Vice President would resign: Hughes would then succeed instantly to the Presidency under the existing law of succession.*

As it turned out, Wilson's narrow victory made the

* By the Presidential Succession Act of January 19, 1886 (repealed in 1947), Congress provided that, in case of the disqualification of both the President and Vice President, the Secretary of State should act as President. Next in the line of succession was the Secretary of the Treasury, and so on down the line of Cabinet members. By the act of July 18, 1947, the Speaker of the House and the President pro tempore of the Senate are put ahead of Cabinet members in the order of succession.

scheme unnecessary. In 1920, however, it might well have been put into effect. Wilson's administration was pinned down by a Republican Congress, the Senate had rejected the Versailles Treaty, and the election of Harding was certainly a rejection of much else that Wilson had stood for. But by this time Wilson was ill and embittered, and he made no effort to revive the resignation plan.

The fiasco of the Hoover-Roosevelt relationship in 1932–33 contributed to further realization of the danger of the slow turnover. From this experience did come the precedent that in troubled times the President and President-elect should meet and confer on the nation's problems; but the experience also suggested the limited accomplishment that could be expected from such talks. Hoover was anxious for Roosevelt's co-operation in the economic crisis, but since the President was on the scene and confident that he *knew* what had to be done, his idea of co-operation was that Roosevelt should join in supporting Hoover's policies. F.D.R. was preoccupied with Cabinet-building and uncertain of what course he wanted to follow, but he was sure that he did not want to bail out Hoover in a way that would commit him later on.

While Hoover and Roosevelt were fencing, Congress was having what was to be its last lame-duck session. Senator George W. Norris, a progressive Republican from Nebraska, had long been outraged by goings-on in these sessions and had been trying to do something about them. Earlier in 1932 his constitutional amendment, bottled up by the Republican leadership for ten years, had finally been approved by the Democratic Congress, and by February, 1933, enough states had ratified it. The Twentieth Amendment's principal feature was a provision that the terms of representatives and senators begin and end at noon on January 3 rather than in March, and that annual sessions of Congress begin at the same time. Thus congressmen elected in November would take their seats eight weeks later, and there would be no more lame-duck sessions—unless the President called a special session to run between Election Day and January. The amendment also shortened the presidential interval by moving Inauguration Day up from March 4 to January 20. The period from January 3 to 20 was allowed for Congress to count the electoral votes and resolve the contest in the event that two candidates tied or that none received a majority. The congressional schedule was the main thing in the minds of the amendment's supporters, and shortening the presidential interval from sixteen to ten weeks was a handy extra. Perhaps, if the amendment had been written after rather than before the Hoover-Roosevelt affair, a more drastic curtailment of the interval might have been attempted.

Since World War II there has been a rapid growth of customs and devices for helping bridge the power gap between Presidents. Every administration now offers briefings on the military and foreign situation to the candidates of all major parties. If the President is retiring or has been defeated, he invites the President-elect to the White House for conferences, and arrangements for communication between the incoming and outgoing regimes are carefully worked out. Instead of waiting until the eve of inauguration to announce the Cabinet, as in the old days, modern Presidents-elect are urged to hasten the announcement of their principal appointees, so that these men can begin familiarizing themselves with their duties and selecting their own subordinates. In 1952, for example, Dwight Eisenhower had announced all of his Cabinet appointments by December 1, and in 1960 John Kennedy had completed the job, after a remarkably effective search for talent, by December 17. Men designated for Cabinet and other high offices customarily are invited to confer and even take up quarters in the agencies they will head, well in advance of the inauguration. Task forces are put to work refining campaign promises into specific proposals that the new President can make to Congress shortly after he takes office.

Congress in 1964 passed a Presidential Transition Act which formally declares that orderly transitions in the office of President are required by the national interest. All officers of the government are instructed to take appropriate action to that end. The law also recognizes one of the problems in such efforts—the substantial expenses of the President-elect and the Vice President-elect and of their embryonic administration during a period when they are still technically private citizens—and authorizes the expenditure of up to $900,000 in public funds for such items as rent, telephones, travel, and staff salaries to aid the President-elect's preparations. To avoid waiting for the electoral votes to be cast and counted, which would defeat the purpose of the act, the Administrator of General Services is authorized to ascertain the "apparently successful candidates" and start providing resources to them after the general election. This law will get its first practical test in 1968–69.

In recent years Congress has given passing consideration to various proposals for further shortening the interval between the election and the inauguration. Most of these have been mixed up with plans for abolishing or changing the basis of voting in the Electoral College, plans which have such potentiality for redistribution of political power in the nation that Congress has been unable or unwilling to act. Yet even if the electoral vote mechanism were retained, modern conditions of communication and transportation would make it technically possible to install a President ten days after the popular votes were cast. Most of the proposals have been a little more cautious, allowing generally a month for the settling of electoral contests and for the President-elect to prepare himself. One of the more sensible of these proposals calls for moving Election Day up to early October, beginning congressional terms in early November, and inaugurating the President a week later—a scheme that would make for better adjustment both to the necessities of the government's fiscal-year cycle and to the schedules of travel, school terms, and vacations that prevail in the United States.

Yet despite their theoretical desirability and technical feasibility, proposals to chop the awkward interval to a month or less come up against a couple of practical realities of politics and human affairs. First (and less important) is that it takes an outgoing administration a few weeks to wind up loose ends and prepare to transfer responsibilities to other hands; the alternative is to pass a great deal of untidy and unfinished business on to successors who will not be able to deal with it as effectively as the outgoing group. More important is the fact that, unlike the British, the American political party system does not keep a

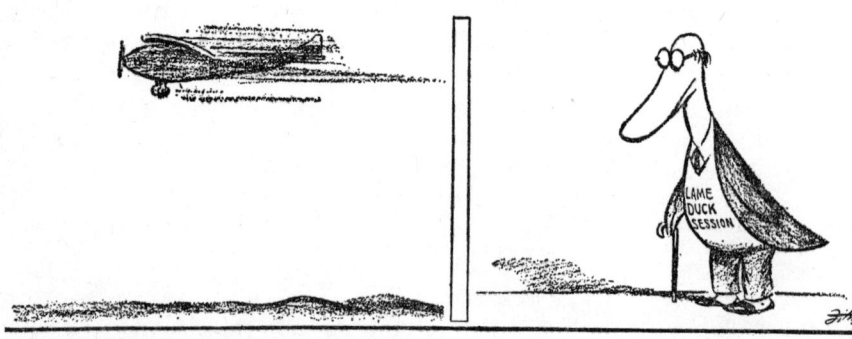

To-day we can travel 200 miles an hour, but—

We keep this dodo because Congressmen rode on horseback 150 years ago.

The Then and Now of a Lame-Duck Congress

Lame-duck sessions of Congress were eliminated in 1933 by the Twentieth Amendment, which also advanced the presidential inauguration day from March to January. Cartoonists did their part in the agitation to promote the change, often stressing the idea that modern transportation had made the old system a silly and wasteful anomaly.

shadow cabinet organized and waiting to put long-agreed-on policies into effect on short notice if the electoral decision is favorable. An American President-elect has to collect his men from disparate fields, many of them outside active politics, and together they must inform themselves, learn to co-operate, and negotiate toward policies that will be both practical and politically acceptable. Pushing a new President and his administration into official responsibility prematurely, before they are properly informed and organized, might hold more dangers for the nation than the custodianship of a lame duck.

In 1948 Governor Thomas E. Dewey, who confidently expected to win the Presidency, began making visible preparations during the campaign and was reported (although he never admitted it) to have already selected a Cabinet. After Truman's upset victory, Dewey was razzed for his premature planning, and it has since become an item of American political lore that the candidate must not appear so overconfident or presumptuous. Nevertheless, John Kennedy in 1960 did make some quiet and limited preparations during the campaign that later served him well: on the day after his election he was able to announce that Clark Clifford was handling transitional relationships with the Eisenhower administration and that Professor Richard Neustadt was working on organization of a White House staff. Kennedy's famous "talent scout" operation was in high gear shortly thereafter. There is reason to hope that both the Democratic and the Republican candidates in this year's election already have lists of potential key assistants, in their minds if not in their pockets. Even without basic reforms in the American party system, such forehandedness by candidates can and no doubt will be intensified in future years.

Since Hoover, we have not had a President directly rejected for re-election. Like Lyndon Johnson, Harry S. Truman retired voluntarily in a year when his prospects were not good, and Dwight D. Eisenhower came up against the two-term limitation on the Presidency enacted by the Twenty-second Amendment. Both Truman and Eisenhower managed their departures in good form and made serious efforts to preserve continuity in the effectiveness of the Presidency. Yet, although neither suffered as much as Hoover, each experienced what might be identified as the lame-duck syndrome—loss of power in the administrative extremities, a feeling of futility in foreign relations, an irresistible urge to push ahead with projects that could not possibly succeed, and wistful hopes that his designated successor would step forward to defend his positions.

Truman, for example, was proud of his efforts to achieve an orderly transition, and on the basis of this he presumed to give Dutch-uncle lectures to Eisenhower, who had just won in an electoral landslide. Although Truman insisted that he remained fully responsible for conducting the nation's affairs until January 20, he put pressure on Eisenhower to support the administration's position on a sticky point in the armistice negotiations then going on with North Korea. Again, while he knew Eisenhower had promised to give title to the disputed offshore oil lands to the states, Truman defiantly signed an eleventh-hour executive order proclaiming the tidelands as naval petroleum reserves in an open reminder to the Republicans of the old scandals of Teapot Dome. (The order was revoked by the new Republican Congress.)

During Eisenhower's last year in the White House, he managed to defend his domestic policy by threatening or actually exercising the veto, but he found himself at a standstill in foreign relations. After the U-2 affair, Khrushchev broke up a summit conference at Paris and sat down to wait for the next President. Ike suffered the further humiliation of having to call off a trip to Japan after he was already on the way: the prospect of his visit was causing civil disorder in Tokyo. After Kennedy had been elected, Eisenhower became concerned about the outflow of gold from the United States and sent the Secretary of the Treasury on a well-publicized mission to Germany in an effort to persuade the Germans to bear some of the expense of maintaining American troops there. Before he left, the Secretary sought Kennedy's blessing for the mission. Kennedy fobbed him off on a subordinate and avoided any commitment. The Germans, of course, proved to be uninterested in dealing with an outgoing administration on so touchy a matter.

Such lame-duckish behavior is easy enough to criticize after the fact, but there remains a serious dilemma: for a period of ten weeks the President is responsible but cannot lead; the President-elect, on the other hand, has influence but neither responsibility nor access to the levers of policy execution. Unfortunately, foreign and domestic crises have no regard for the electoral calendar. Responsible conduct by the outgoing President, rapid preparations by the President-elect, and sensible understandings between incoming and outgoing regimes can help guard the nation—but only drastic shortening could alleviate the awkward interval.

Mr. Henry is a professor of government and foreign affairs at the University of Virginia. He has been a consultant to various agencies of the federal government, and is the author of Presidential Transitions, *published in 1960.*

DRAWN BY BLAKE HAMPTON

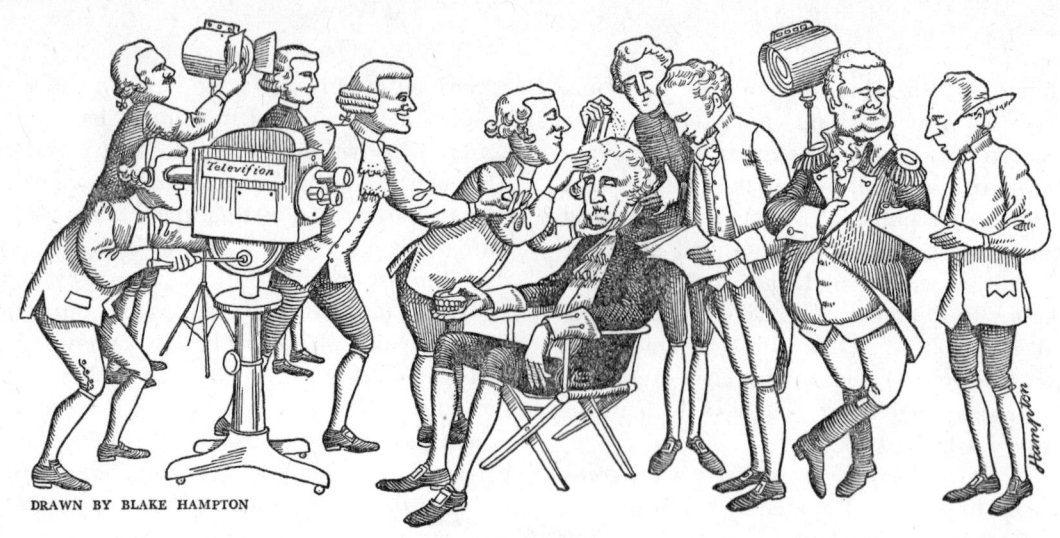

A Backward Look at the New Politics

There has been much talk, during the current presidential campaign, about "the new politics." This phenomenon depends largely on the candidates' voluble entry into your living room by way of the TV set, larger than life and, they hope, twice as natural. Few of the people who voted for or against Abe Lincoln ever got close enough to him to see what he really looked like in action, whereas in this election, if the Republican candidate doesn't shave closely enough, or the Democratic candidate develops a nervous facial tic, everyone knows about it.

This electronic intimacy, the theory goes, has brought a new quality into presidential politics. Looks and personality may count more than reputation or, for that matter, actual executive ability. For the first time in history a man's political future may hinge on the same things that make a soap commercial a success or failure—as if, you might say, there were a Tide in the affairs of men.

It is interesting to speculate how some of our earlier Chief Executives might have come off under the exposure of the new politics. As a test case, let us consider the following scene in which the Father of his Country is preparing for a television appearance.

Scene: *President Washington's office, October, 1792. As a crew of technicians hustles about the room adjusting lights and other equipment, a make-up man, Secretary of the Treasury Alexander Hamilton, and Secretary of War Henry Knox hover around Washington, who is taking his seat in front of the camera.*

MAKE-UP MAN. General, I think just a *touch* of the brush on the bridge of your nose would put the finish on it. It cuts down the reflection a bit. You have, if I may say so, Sir, a . . . a *magnificent* nose.

WASHINGTON. Well, well, do it and be done with it! I reiterate that all this falderal over appearances, in my estimation, is a pack of stuff and nonsense. A man is, sir, what he is. How many people did you say will be watching tonight, Henry?

KNOX. Estimated at four million, sir.

WASHINGTON. Hmmm. Four million. But who are they? Riff-raff, no doubt, for the most part.

HAMILTON. We all know that your people, sir, is a great beast. But as things go in this so-called democracy, sir, this beast can nourish a man or devour him. The beast must be pleased.

WASHINGTON. You have a gift for metaphor, Hamilton. How's my wig?

MAKE-UP MAN. The wig is *perfect*, General. Please remember not to try to adjust it after we go on the air. Don't even *touch* it!

WASHINGTON. Have I got time to take these damnable teeth out for a moment? They hurt my gums.

KNOX. Two minutes to go, General. Take them out for one minute, but make sure to re-set them firmly. Otherwise there is an unhappy sibilance attendant upon your enunciation of the *s*, sir, that the microphone tends to amplify. The sound men don't like that.

WASHINGTON [*false teeth in hand*]. Damn the thound men, thir! They care for nothing but effecth!

TECHNICIAN. One minute! One minute! [*The lights come up, and, looking more lugubrious than usual, Washington pops his teeth back into place. The telecast begins.*] —E. M. Halliday